NEVER LOSE THEORY:

A BREAKTHROUGH IN FOREX TRADING

Dr. NASSER AFIFY

CONTENTS

Introduction…………….....………………………………………..3

   The First Strategy (pending orders) ………………...…..5

   Buy Stop Orders………….............. ………………………….5

   Sell Stop Orders ....……..……...………….16

   Taking Profits ………………..…………………..………………35

   Probabilities of Profit And Loss................. ………..…38

   The Second Strategy (Instant Execution Orders)……..…40

The First Ten Orders......... ....………………………40

The Second Ten Orders.............. ....………………..60

Taking Profits..…………………..77

Probabilities of Profit And Loss…………………….……..79

Conclusion………………………………….……..………….80

Introduction

What goes up must come down. The bullish trend should go down, and the bearish trend should go up. Therefore, we will benefit from the rise and from the drop. This is the crux of the matter.

I think that dealing with Forex is simpler than many think. Because it is simple, in my view, I looked for a simple way to make profit without resorting to stressful studies, complex analyzes, numerous indicators and mathematical calculations that could ultimately lead to catastrophic failure. If technical and fundamental analyzes, indicators and mathematical calculations lead to certain or almost certain results, all Forex traders would be wealthy.

This does not mean that all analyzes, forecasts, mathematical calculations and indicators are false, but they are uncertain. This leads us to say that if these calculations go wrong in most cases, then we may find another way that can make Forex trading simpler, safer and more profitable.

This strategy or theory must be very simple so that it can be used by everyone, whether beginners who do not have enough information or technical ability or professionals who have spent many years roaming deep water.

The suggested strategy can make a profit whether the trend is going up or down without having to predict the direction of the market. Let us now begin to see how this can be achieved.

The First Strategy:

Pending Orders (Buy Stop and Sell Stop)

The strategy of pending orders is to place a set of buy and sell orders (for example, 10-15 orders) through MT4 or MT5 trading program.

Buy Stop Orders

For example, relating to GBPUSD pair, we can place the first pending order (Buy Stop), at 1.2140 with a take profit at 1.2150 after 10 pips or 15 pips, as shown in the figure.

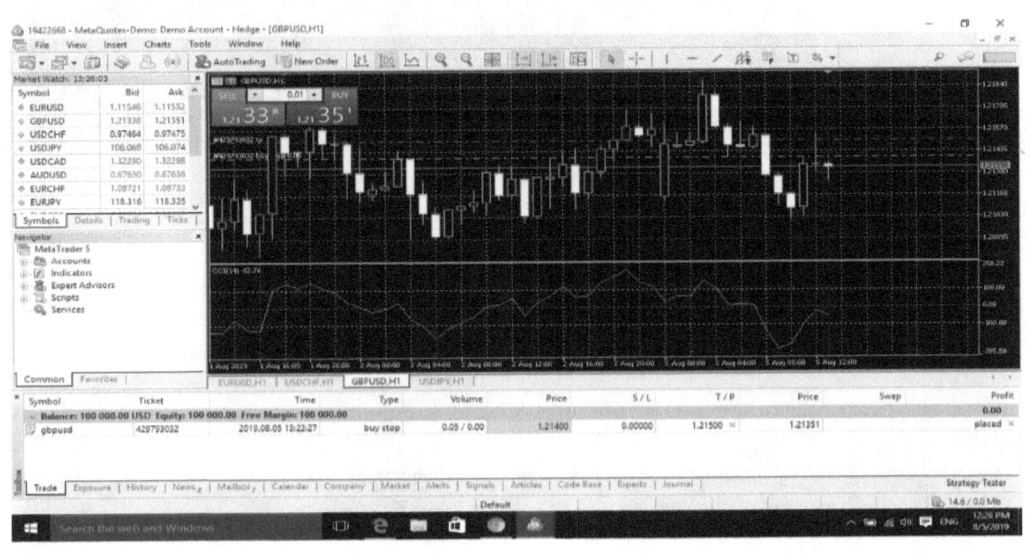

The second pending order is placed after 10 pips at 1.2150 and the Take Profit is placed at 1.2160 or 1.2165.

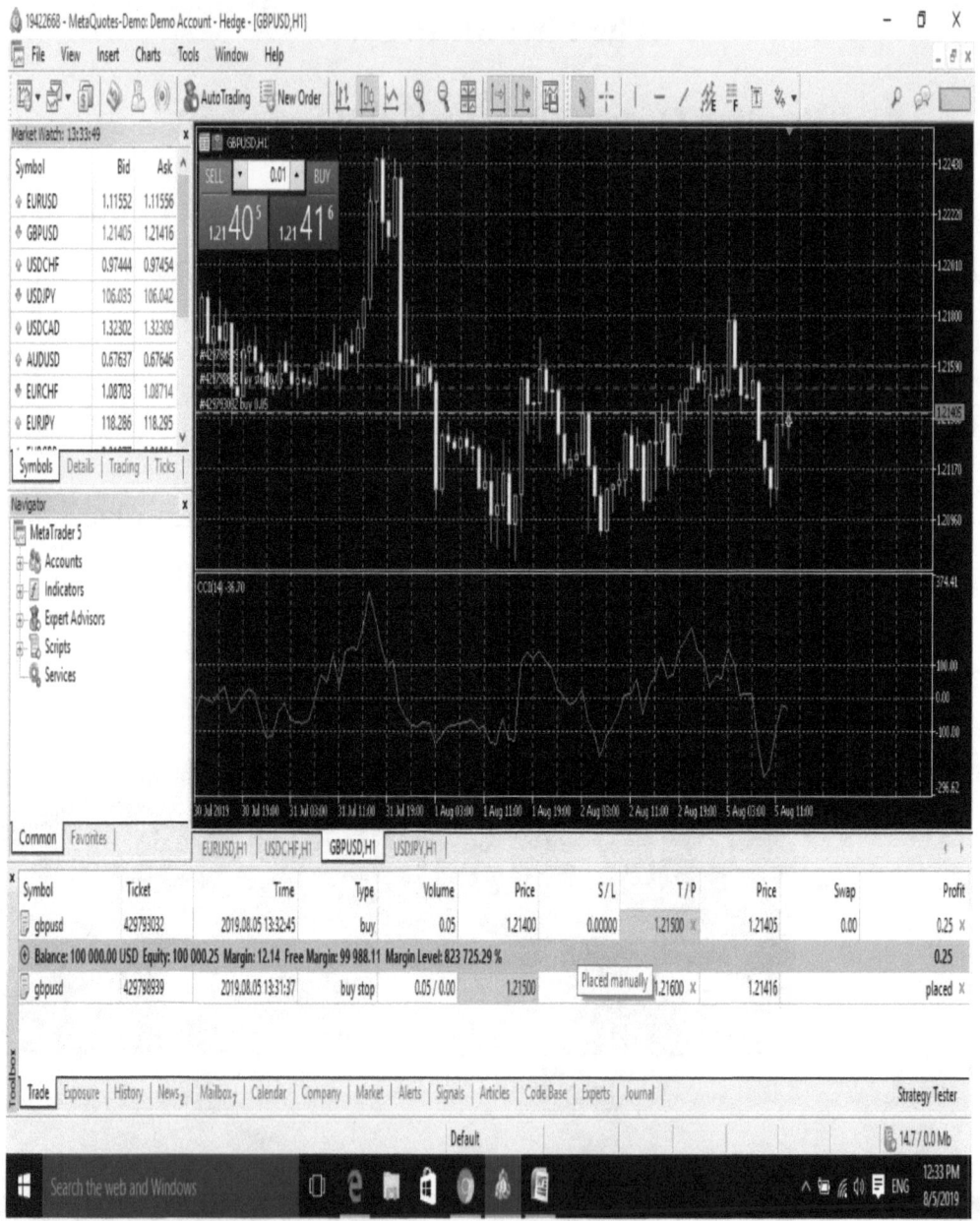

As shown, we have two orders, one is 1.2140 and the second is 1.2150 and the first order has already been executed and started to make profits.

The third buy stop order is placed 10 pips apart from the previous order, i.e. 1.2160 with a take profit limit at 1.2170 or can be placed at 1.2175.

We now have three buy stop orders: 1.2140, 1.2150 and 1.2160, and three profit taking limits which are 1.2150, 1.2160

and 1.2170, so that if the price moves up the orders are executed successively and profits are taken respectively.

The fourth Buy Stop order is placed 10 pips apart from the previous order at 1.2170 with a Take Profit limit at 1.2180 or can be placed at 1.2185.

Now we have four orders, one of which has been executed, 1.2140 and started to make profit as shown and the second one 1.2150 turned green in a sign that it is about to execute. Accordingly, we have four buy stop orders: 1.2140, 1.2150, 1.2160, 1.2170 and four profit taking limits of 1.2150, 1.2160, 1.2170 and 1.2180 respectively.

The fifth pending order is placed 10 pips apart from the previous order at 1.2180 with a take profit limit at 1.2190 or can be placed at 1.2195.

Now we have five orders: 1.2140, 1.2150, 1.2160, 1.2170, 1.2180 and five profit taking limits which are 1.2150, 1.2160, 1.2170, 1.2180 and 1.2190 respectively.

The Sixth Pending Buy Stop order is placed 10 pips apart from the previous order at 1.2190 with a Take Profit limit of 1.2200 or more.

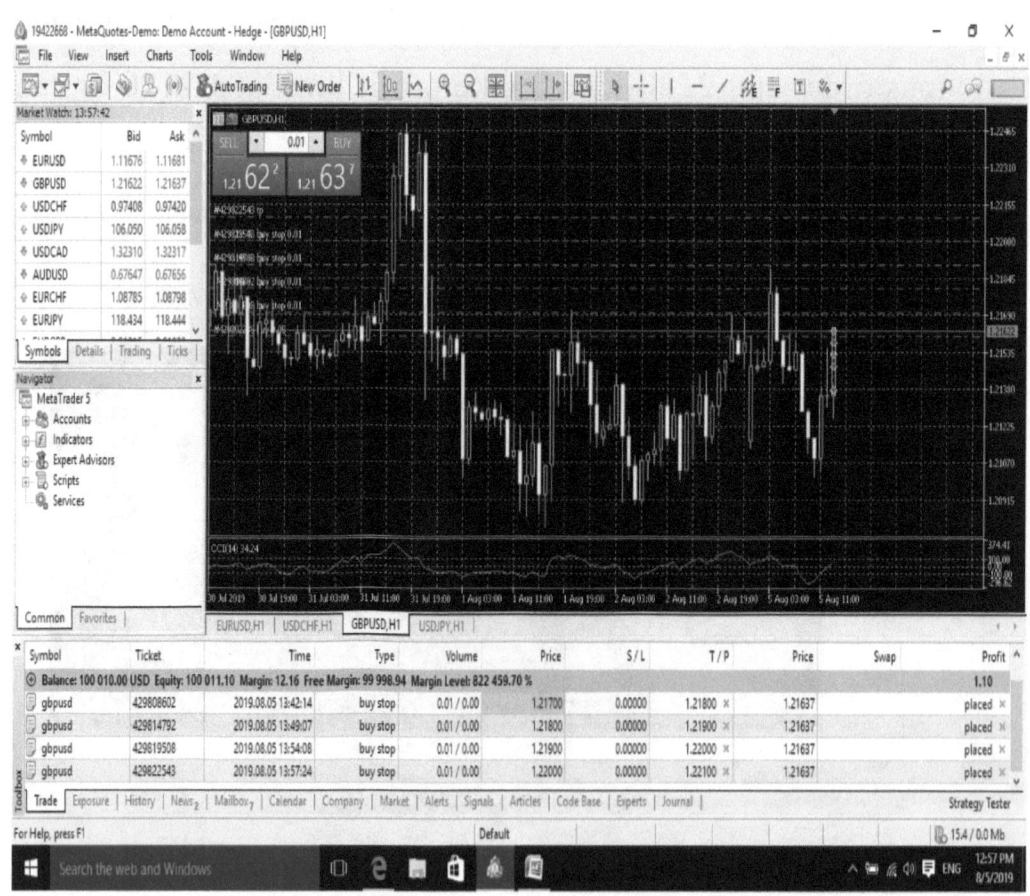

Now we have six orders: 1.2140, 1.2150, 1.2160, 1.2170, 1.2180, 1.2190 and six profit taking limits of 1.2150, 1.2160, 1.2170, 1.2180, 1.2190 and 1.2200 respectively. In the meantime, orders 1.2140 and 1.2150 were executed and closed after profit taking as indicated in the figure.

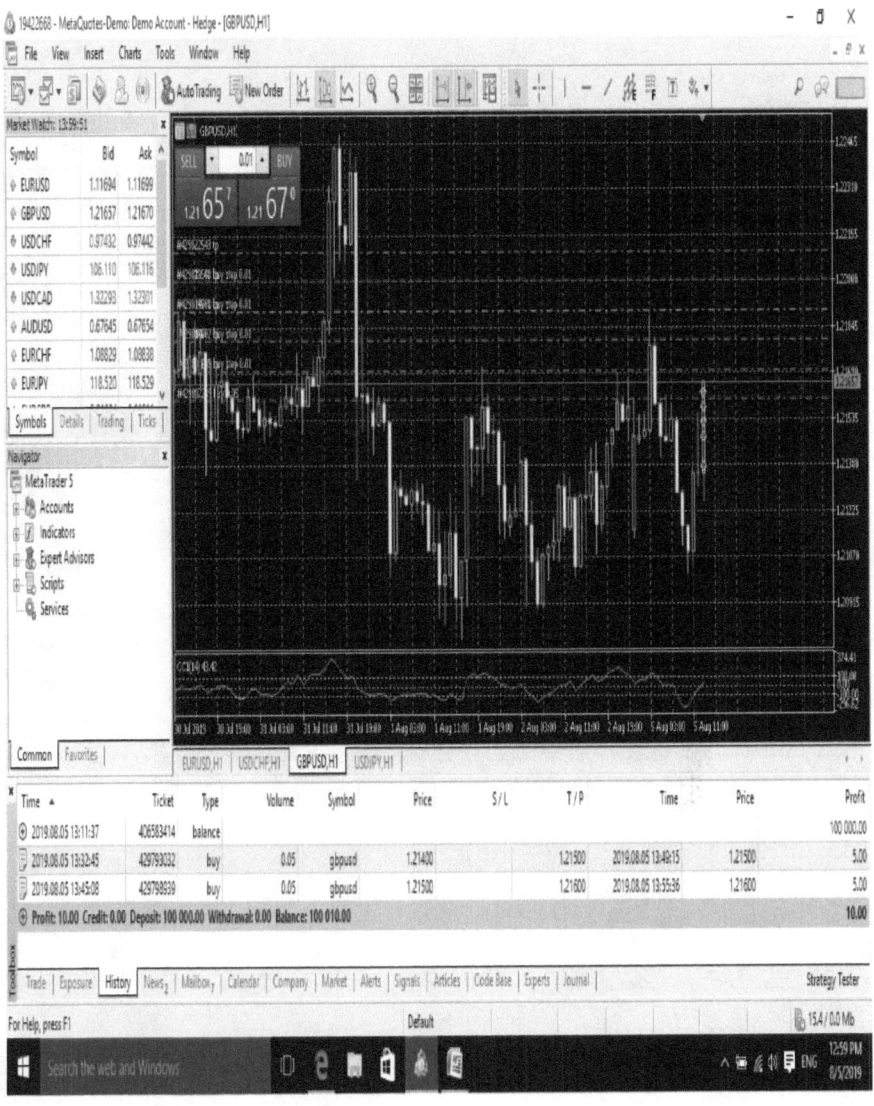

The seventh pending Buy Stop order is placed 10 pips apart from the previous order at 1.2200 with a Take Profit limit of 1.2210 or more.

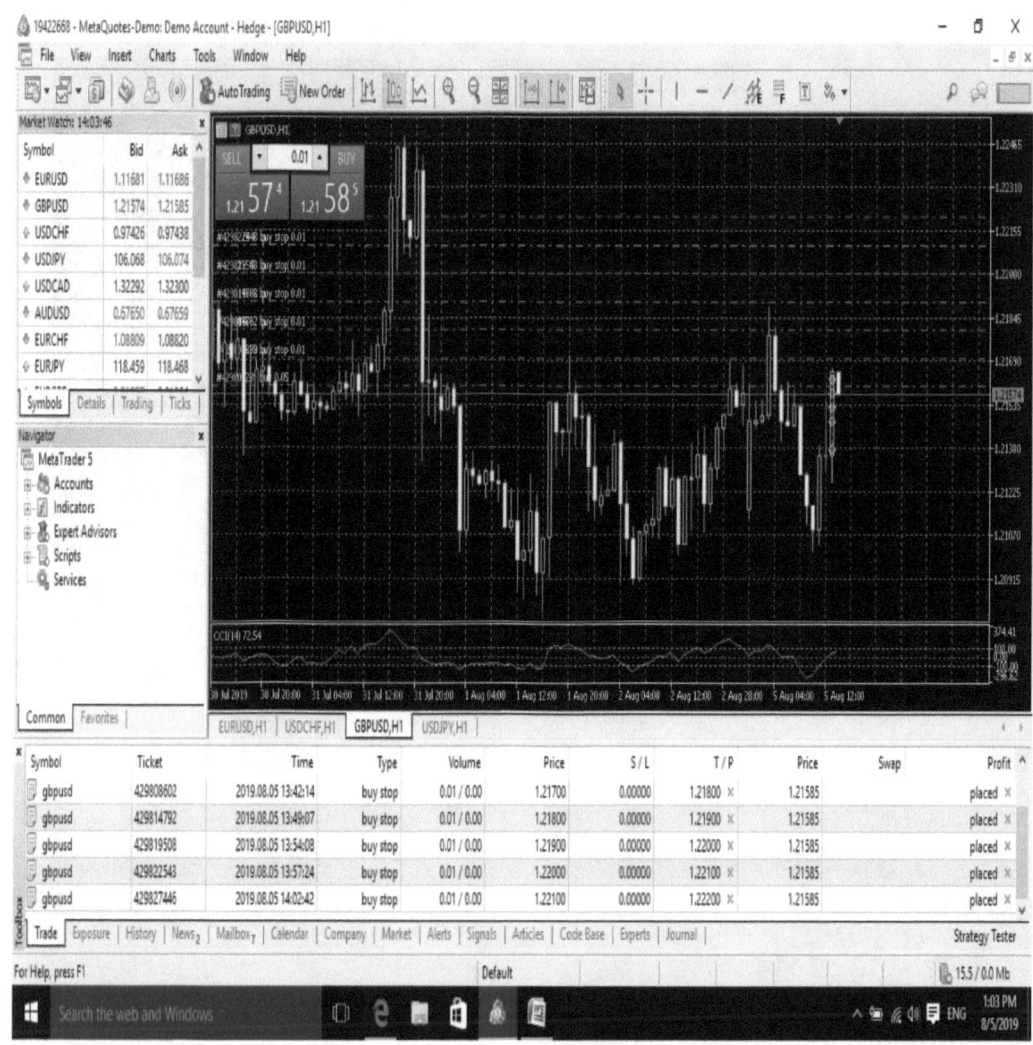

Now we have seven orders: 1.2140, 1.2150, 1.2160, 1.2170, 1.2180, 1.2190, 1.2200 and seven profit-taking limits of 1.2150, 1.2160, 1.2170, 1.2180, 1.2190, 1.2200 and 1.2210 respectively.

The eighth pending order is placed 10 pips apart from the previous order at 1.2210 with a take profit limit at 1.2220 or more.

Now we have eight buy stop orders which are 1.2140, 1.2150, 1.2160, 1.2170, 1.2180, 1.2190, 1.2200, 1.2210 and eight profit-taking limits: 1.2150, 1.2160, 1.2170, 1.2180, 1.2190, 1.2200, 1 .2210 and 1,2220, respectively.

The 9th Pending Buy Stop order is placed 10 pips apart from the previous order at 1.2220 with a Take Profit limit of 1.2230 or more.

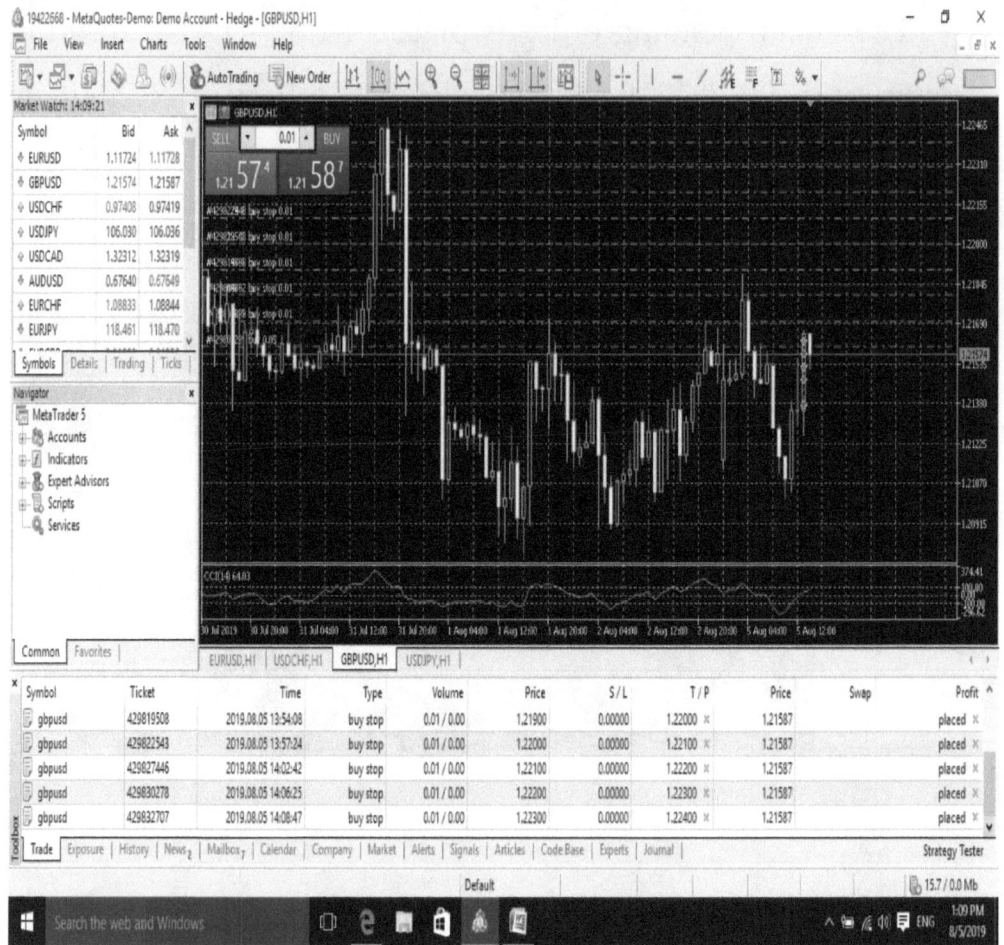

Now we have nine buy orders which are 1.2140, 1.2150, 1.2160, 1.2170, 1.2180, 1.2190, 1.2200, 1.2210, 1.2220 and nine profit taking limits which are 1.2150, 1.2160, 1.2170, 1.2180, 1.2190, 1.2200, 1.2210, 1.2220 and 1.2230, respectively.

The tenth pending buy order is placed 10 pips higher than the previous order at 1.2230 with a take profit limit at 1.2240 or more.

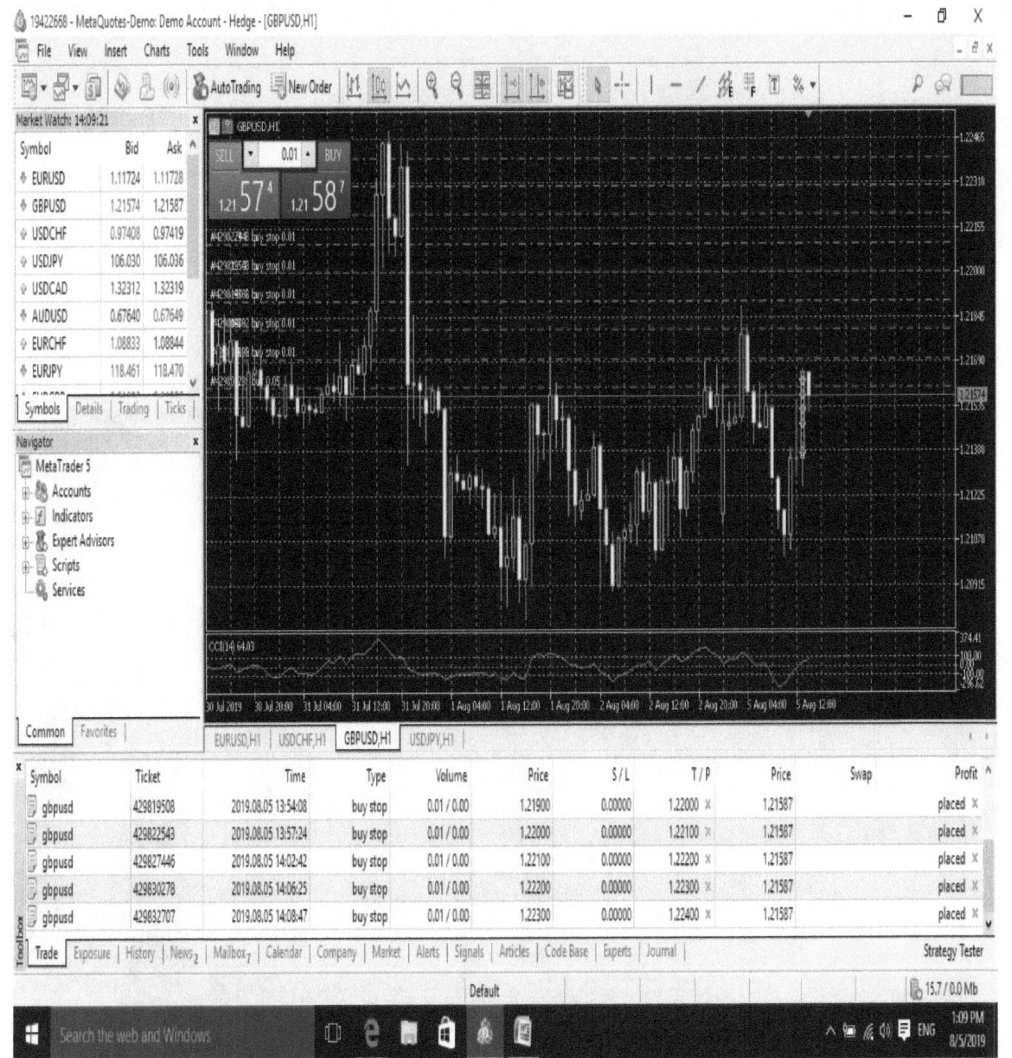

Now we have ten buy stop orders which are 1.2140, 1.2150, 1.2160, 1.2170, 1.2180, 1.2190, 1.2200, 1.2200, 1.2210, 1.2220, 1.2230 and ten profit taking limits which are 1.2150, 1.2160, 1.2170, 1.2180, 2190, 1.2200, 1.2210, 1,2220, 1.2230 and 1.2240 respectively.

Sell Stop Orders

Now that we have placed ten pending buy stop orders, we will place ten sell stop orders. We will place the first sell stop order at 1.2140 with a profit taking limit at 1.2130 as shown.

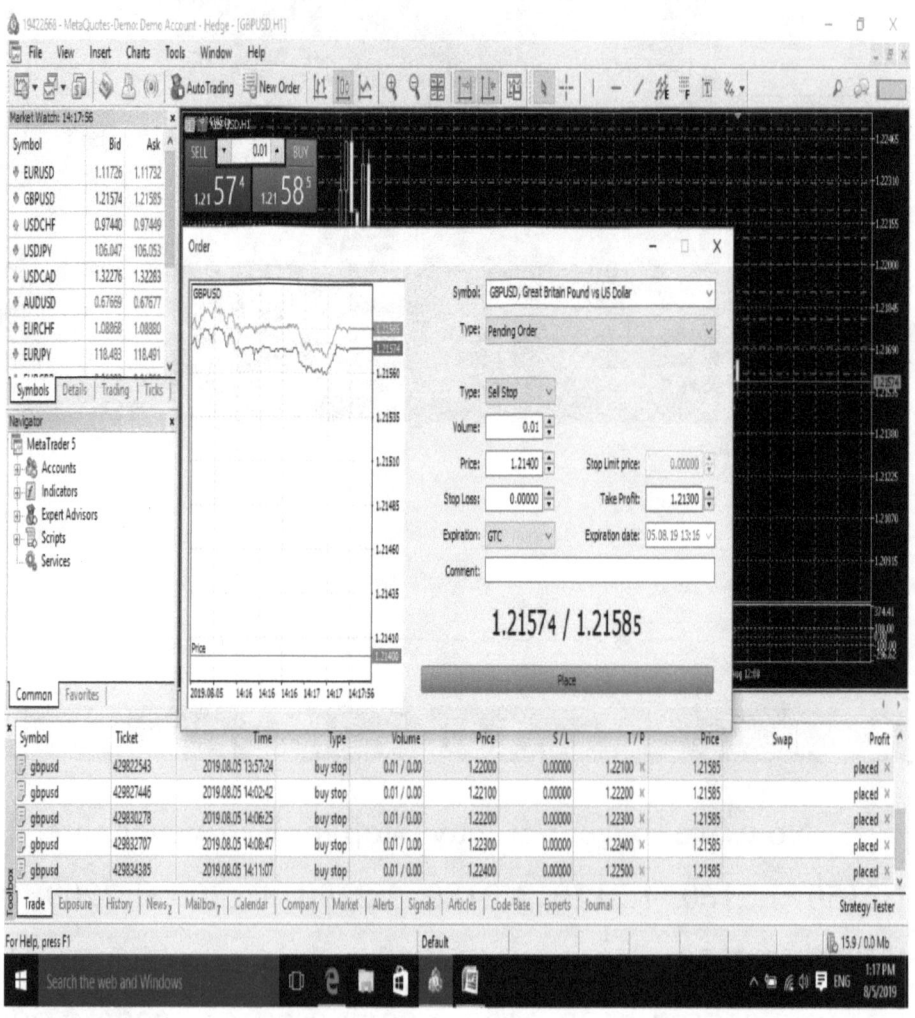

Now we have ten buy stop orders and one sell stop order.

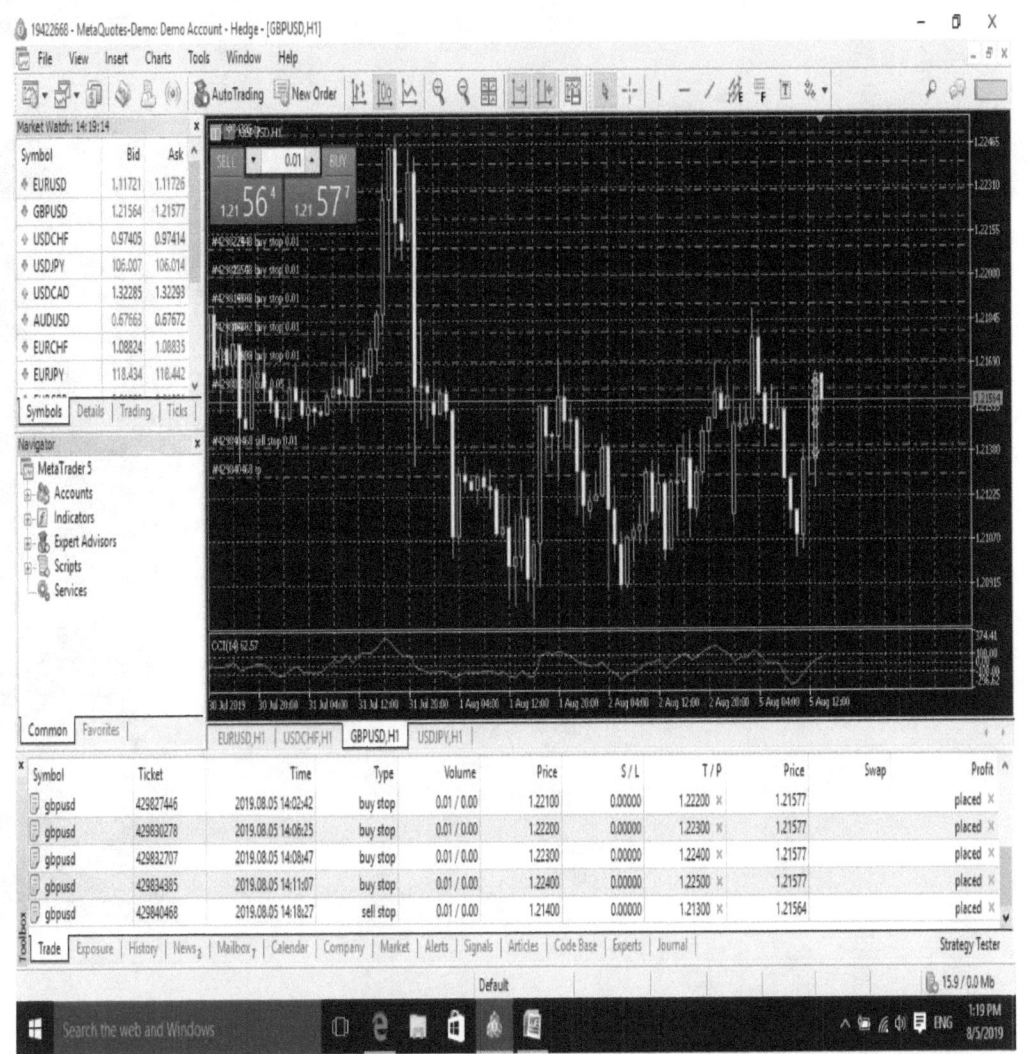

The second pending sell order is placed at 1.2130 and the profit taking limit is placed after 10 pips at 1.2120 as shown.

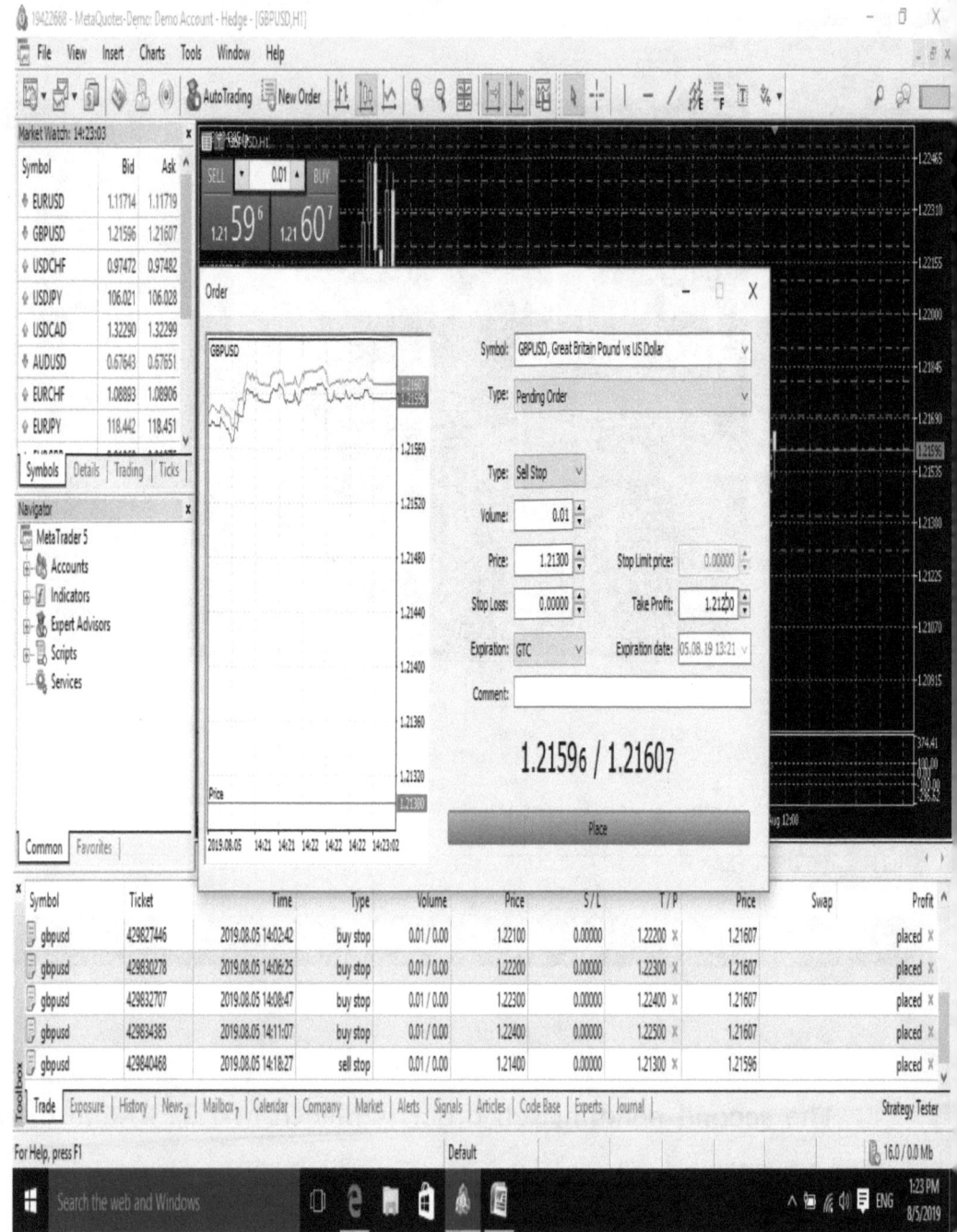

So, we have two pending sell stop orders of 1.2140 and 1.2130 and profit-taking limits of 1.2130 and 1.2120 respectively.

The third pending sell order is placed at 1.2120 and take profit after 10 pips at 1.2110 as shown.

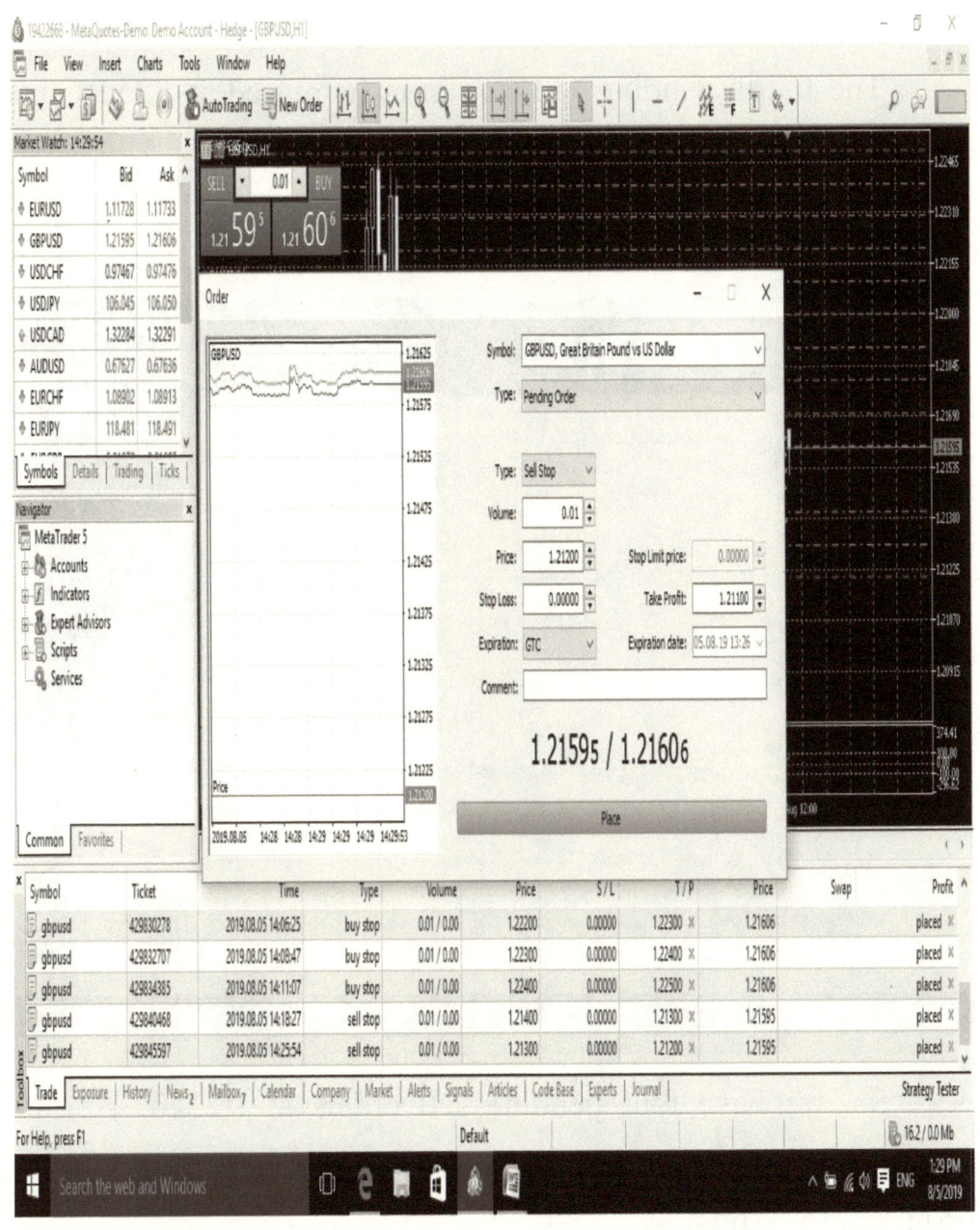

So we have three pending sell stop orders at 1.2140, 1.2130 and 1.2120 and three profit taking limits at 1.2130, 1.2120 and 1.2110 respectively.

The fourth pending sell stop order is placed at 1.2110 and take profit limit after 10 pips at 1.2100 as shown.

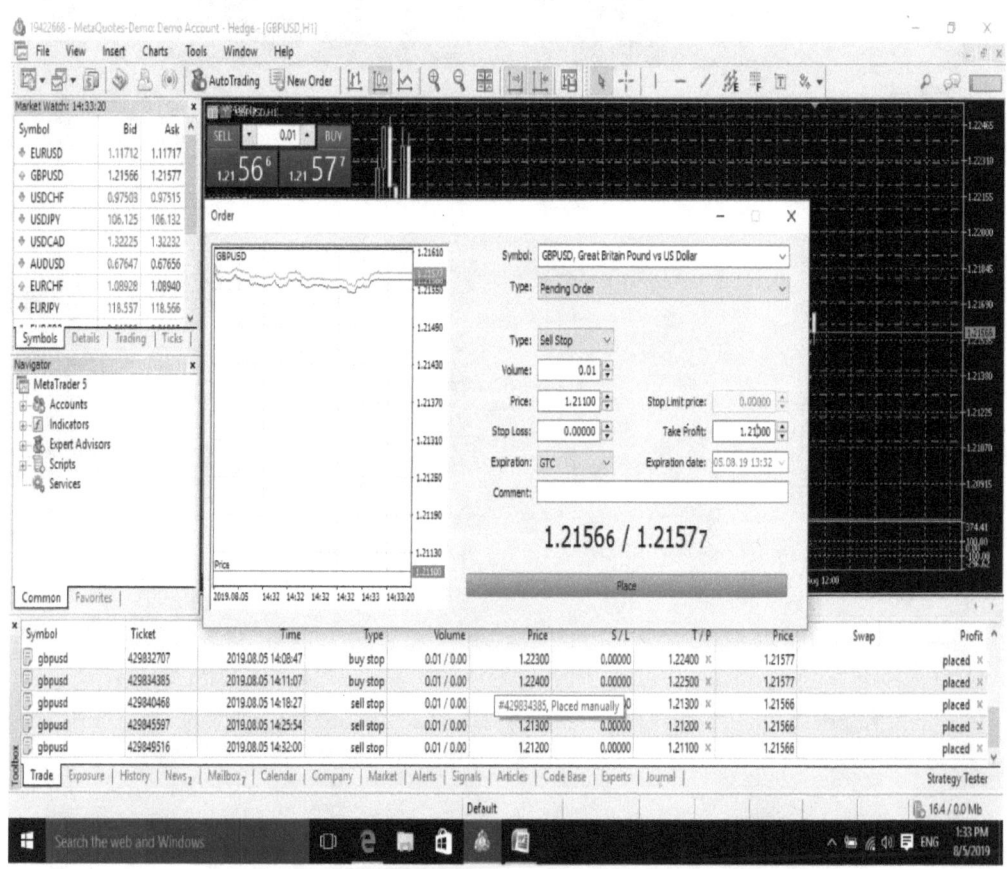

So, we have four pending sell orders at 1.2140, 1.2130, 1.2120 and 1.2110 and four profit taking limits at 1.2130, 1.2120, 1.2110 and 1.2100 respectively.

Pending sell stop orders and take profit limits are shown in the figure.

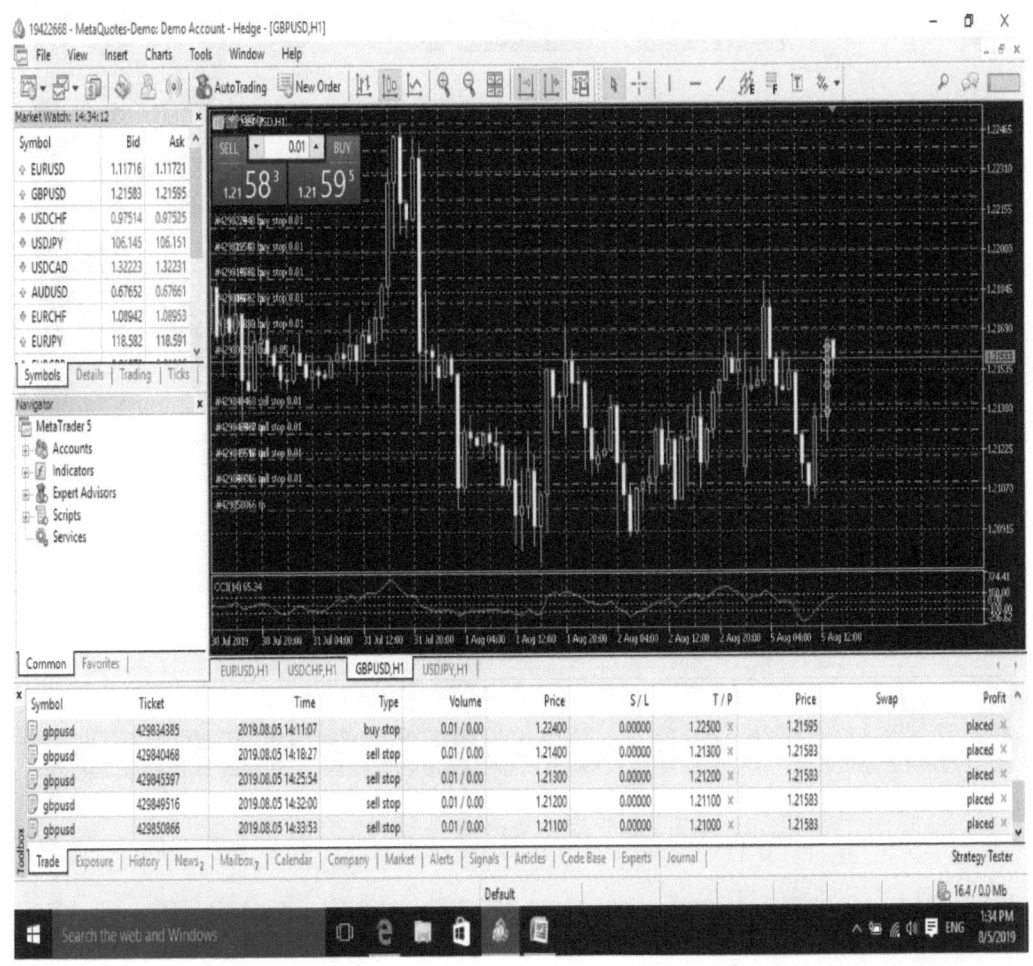

The fifth pending sell stop order is placed at 1.2100 and take profit limit after 10 pips at 1.2090 as shown in figure.

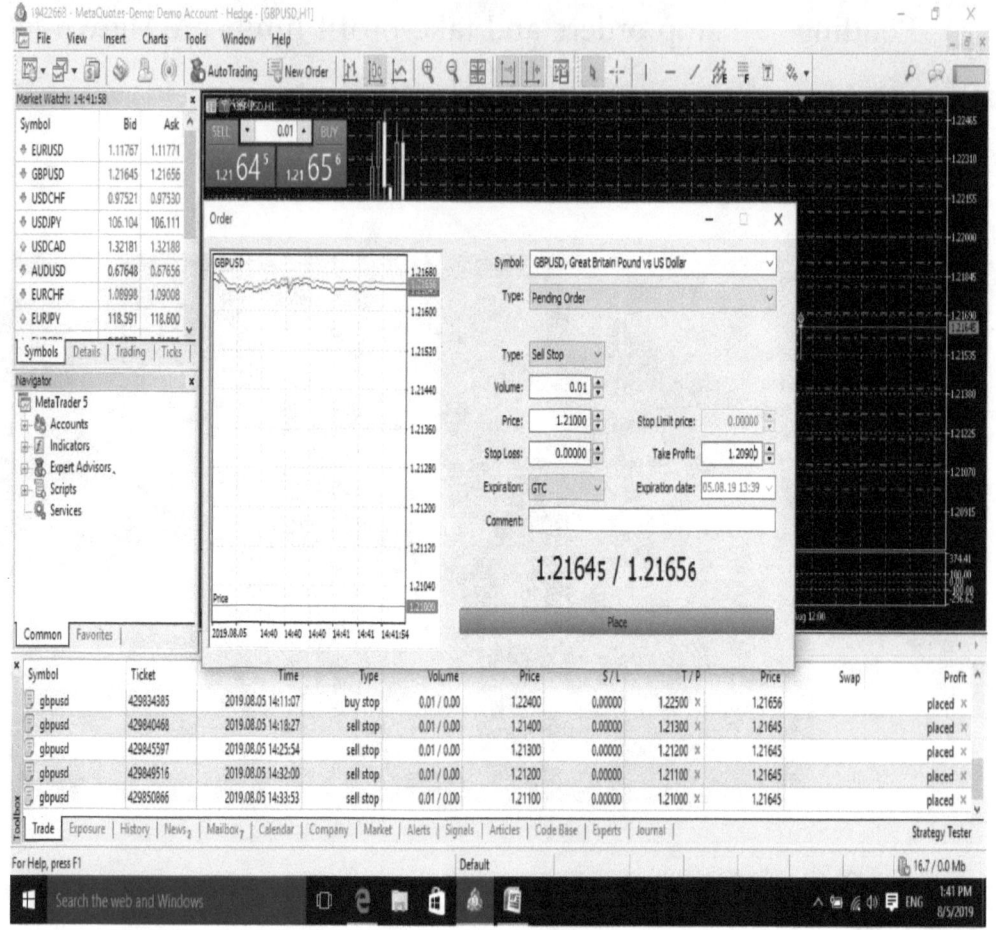

Thus, we have five sell stop orders: 1.2140, 1.2130, 1.2120, 1.2110 and 1.2100 and five profit taking limits at 1.2130, 1.2120, 1.2110, 1.2100 and 1.2090 respectively.

As shown, we now have ten buy stop orders, four of which have been executed, five pending sell stop orders and their profit taking limits.

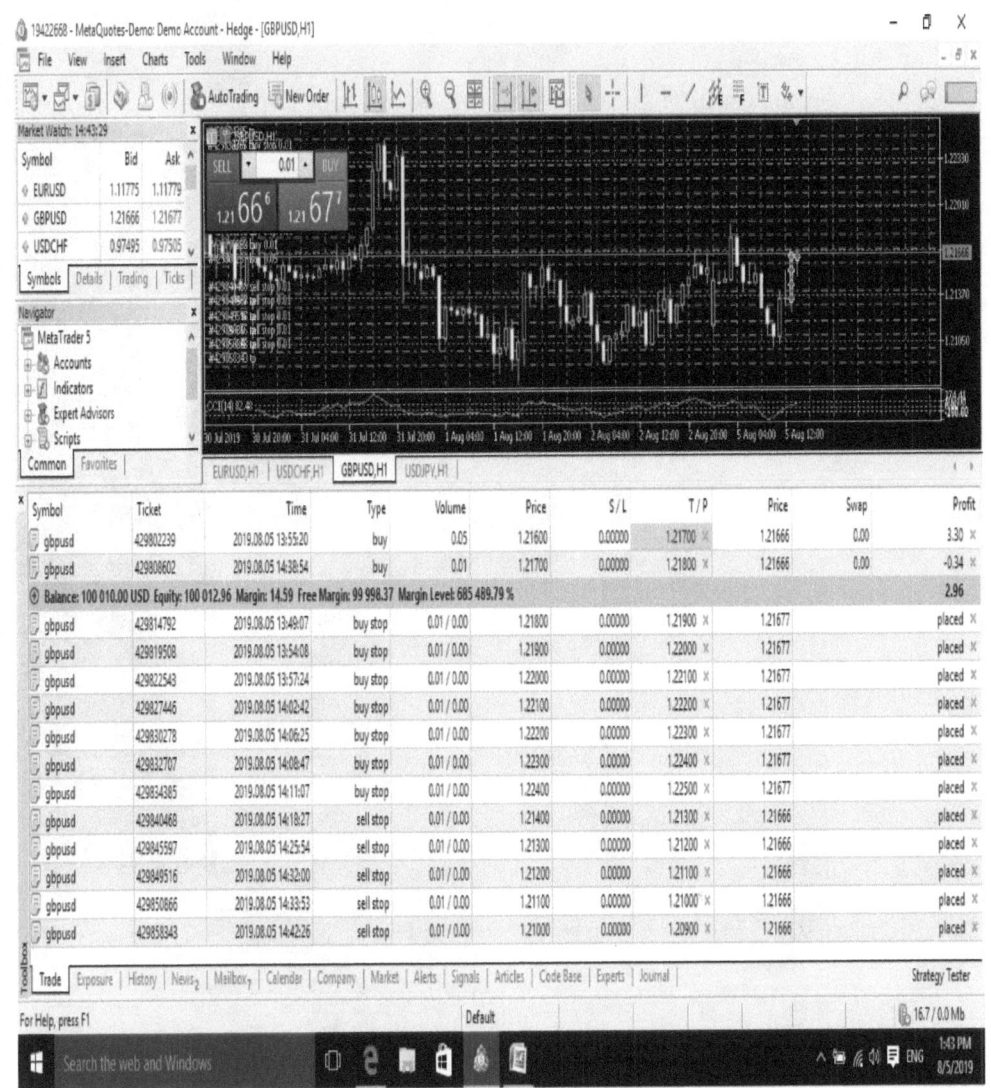

The Sixth Pending Sell stop Order is placed at 1.2090 and Take Profit Limit after 10 pips at 1.2080 as shown.

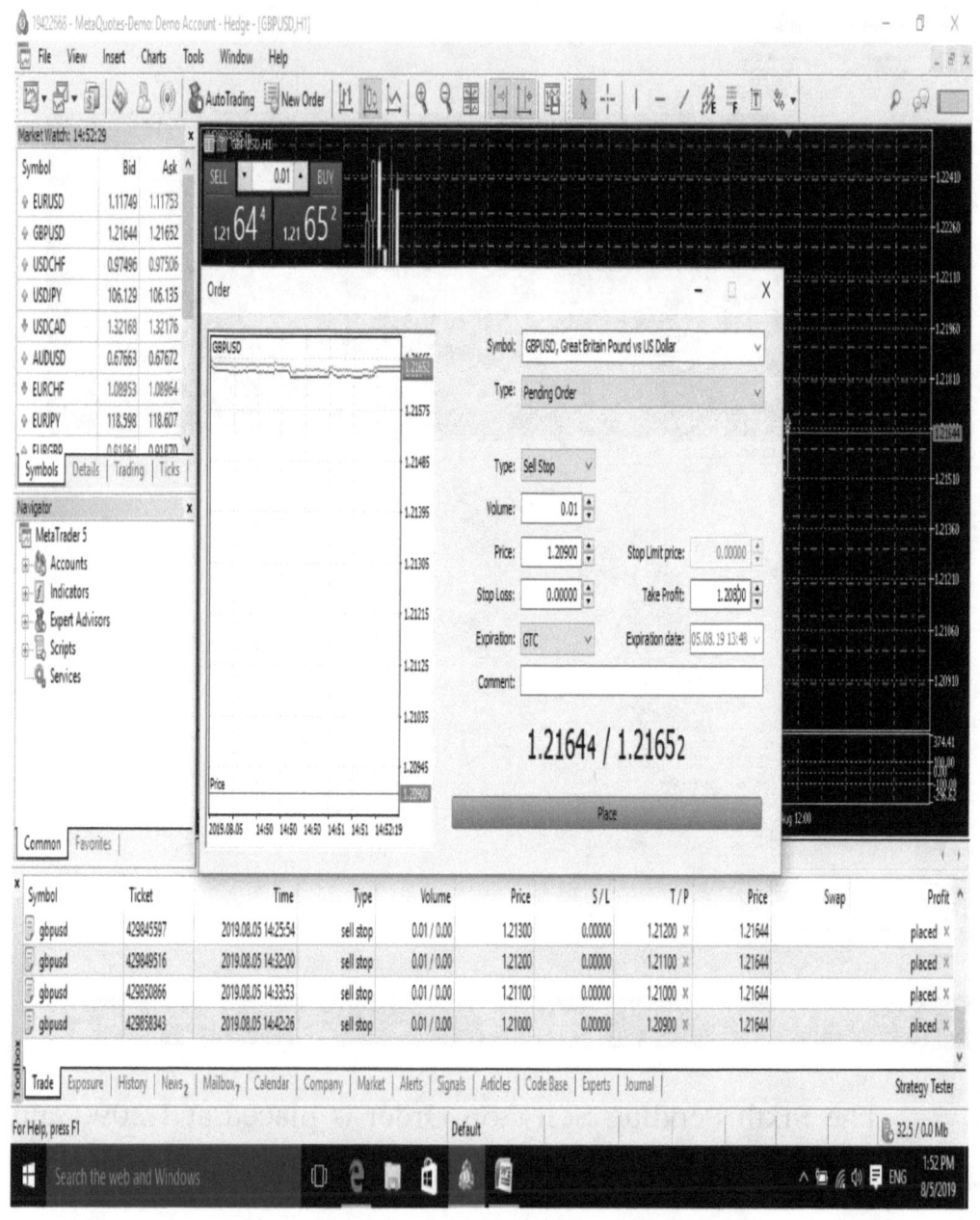

So, we have six pending sell orders: 1.2140, 1.2130, 1.2120, 1.2110, 1.2100 and 1.2090 and six profit taking limits at 1.2130, 1.2120, 1.2110, 1.2100, 1.2090 and 1.2080 respectively.

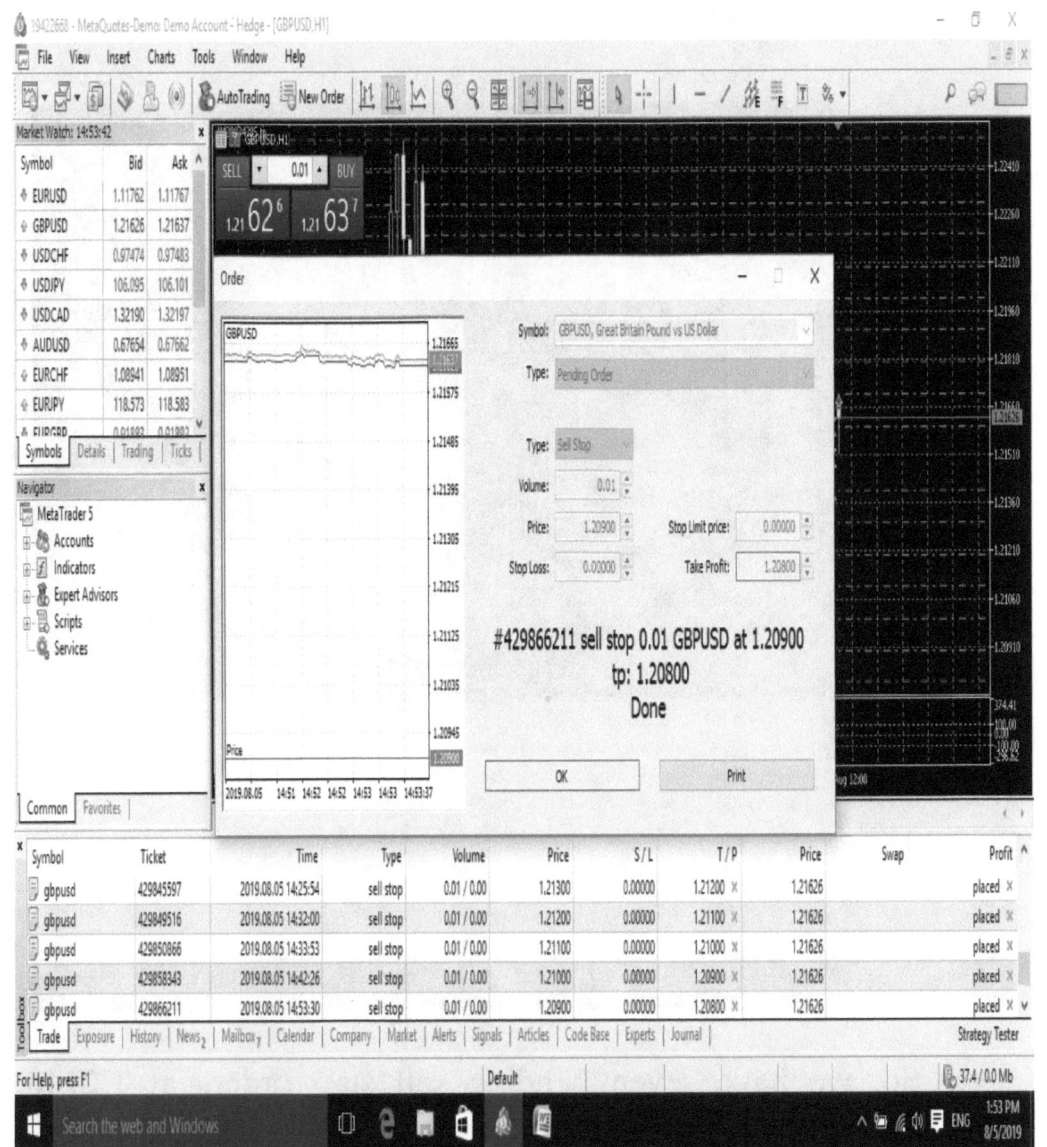

The seventh pending sell stop order is placed at 1.2080 and take profit limit after 10 pips at 1.2070 as shown in the figure.

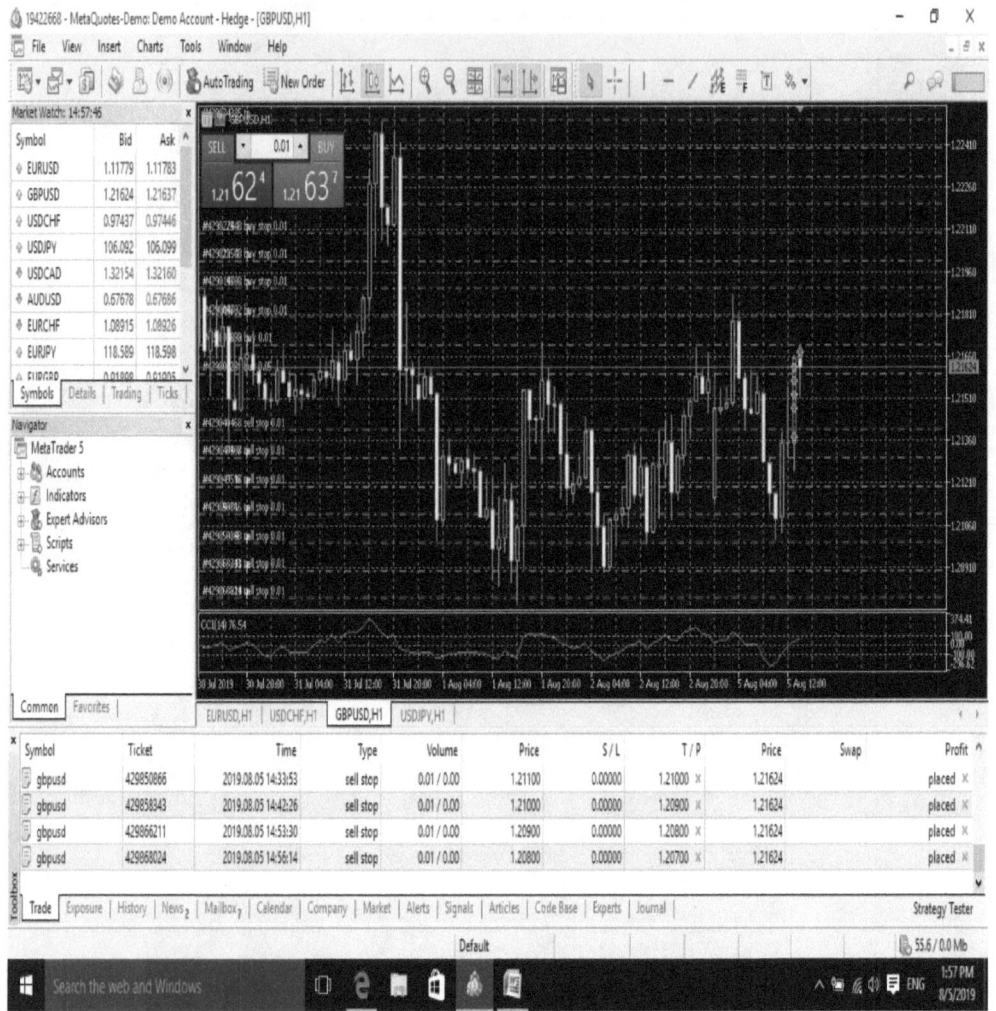

So, we have seven pending sell stop orders at 1.2140, 1.2130, 1.2120, 1.2110, 1.2100, 1.2090 and 1.2080 and seven profit taking limits at 1.2130, 1.2120, 1.2110, 1.2100, 1.2090 and 1.2080 respectively.

The eighth pending sell stop order is placed at 1.2070 and the take profit limit is placed after 10 pips at 1.2060 as shown in the figure.

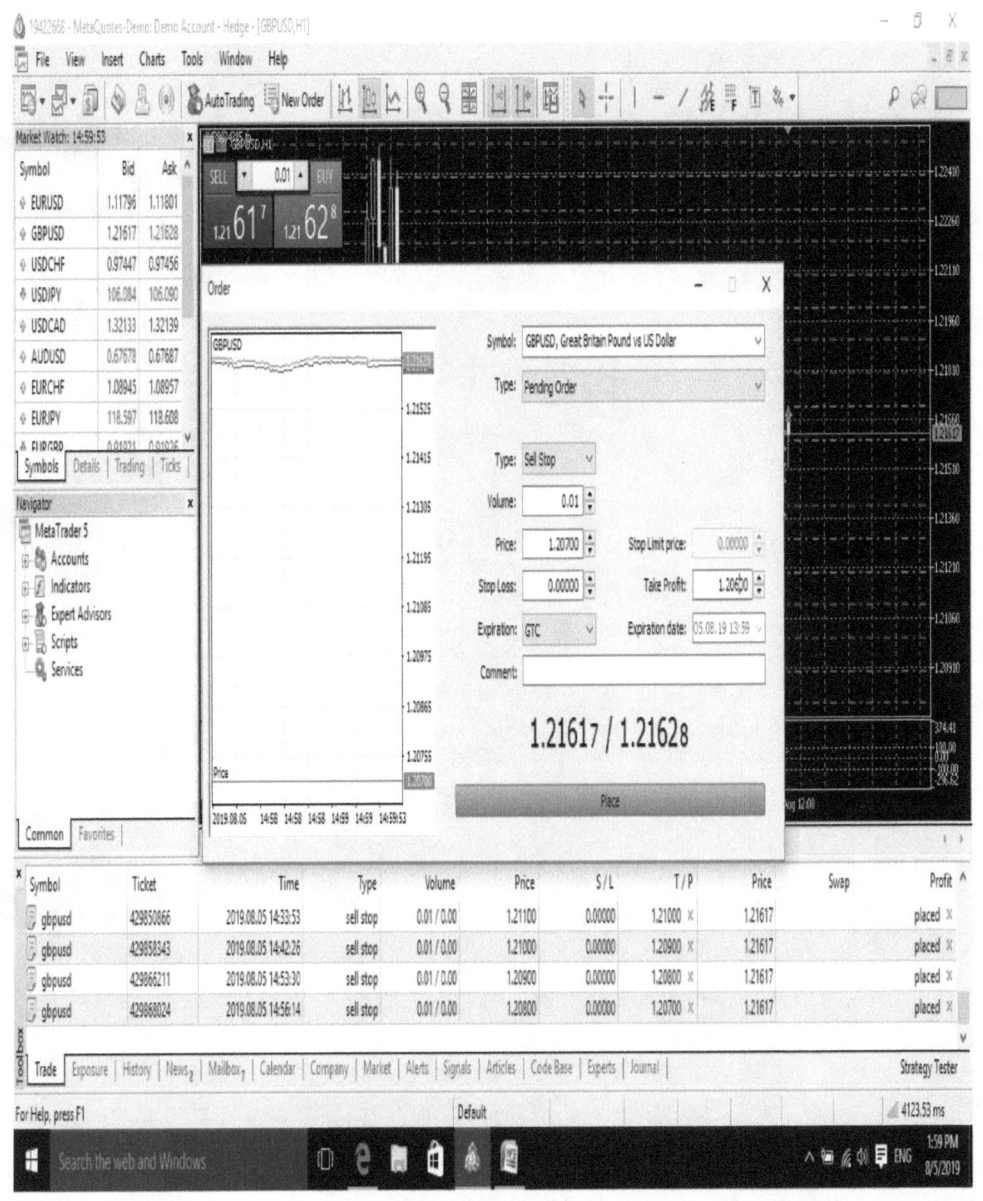

Thus, we have eight pending sell orders: 1.2140, 1.2130, 1.2120, 1, 2110, 1.2100, 1.2090, 1.2080 and 1.2070 and eight profit-taking limits: 1.2130, 1.2120, 1.2110, 1.2100, 1.2090, 1. 2080, 1.2070 and 1.2060 respectively.

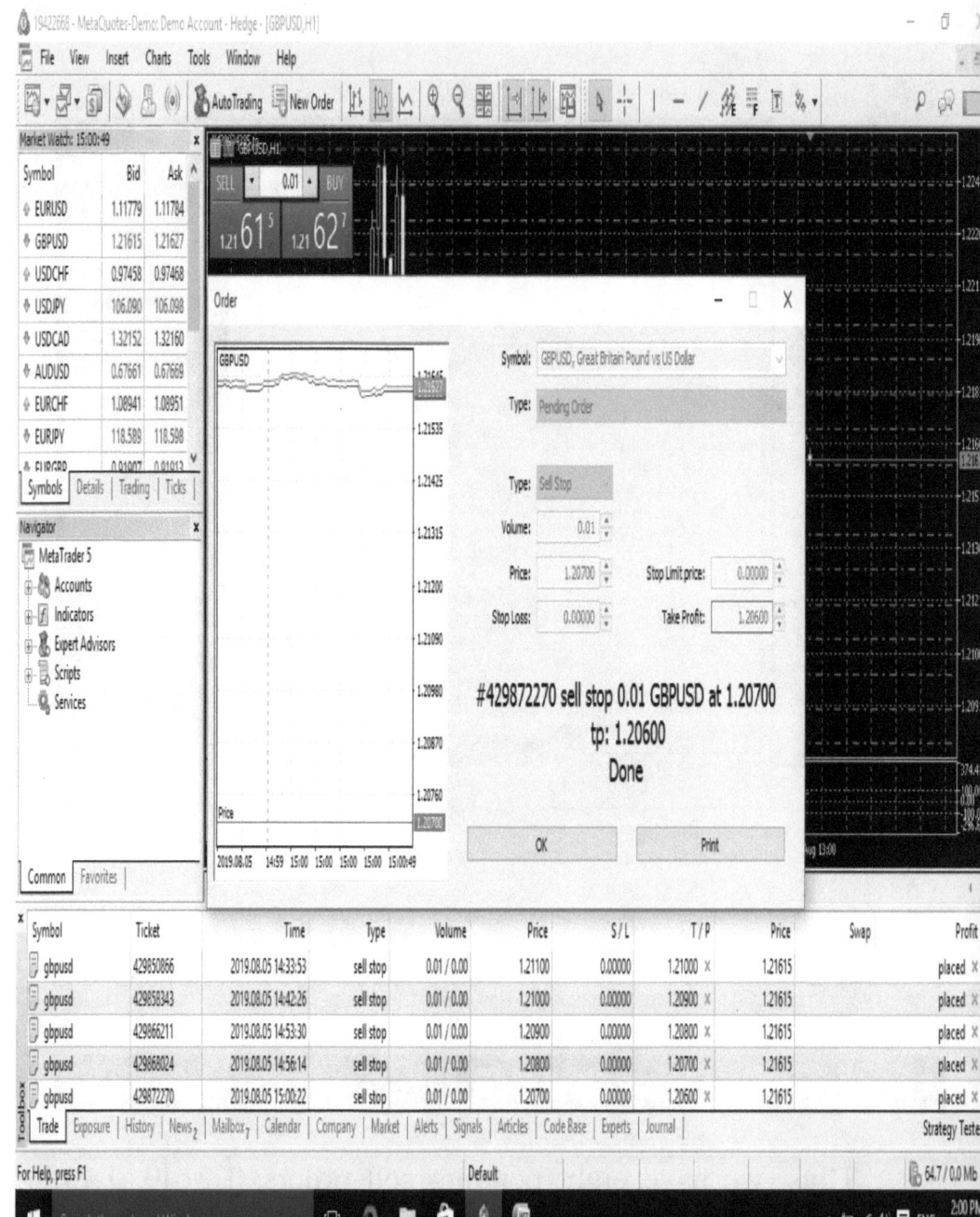

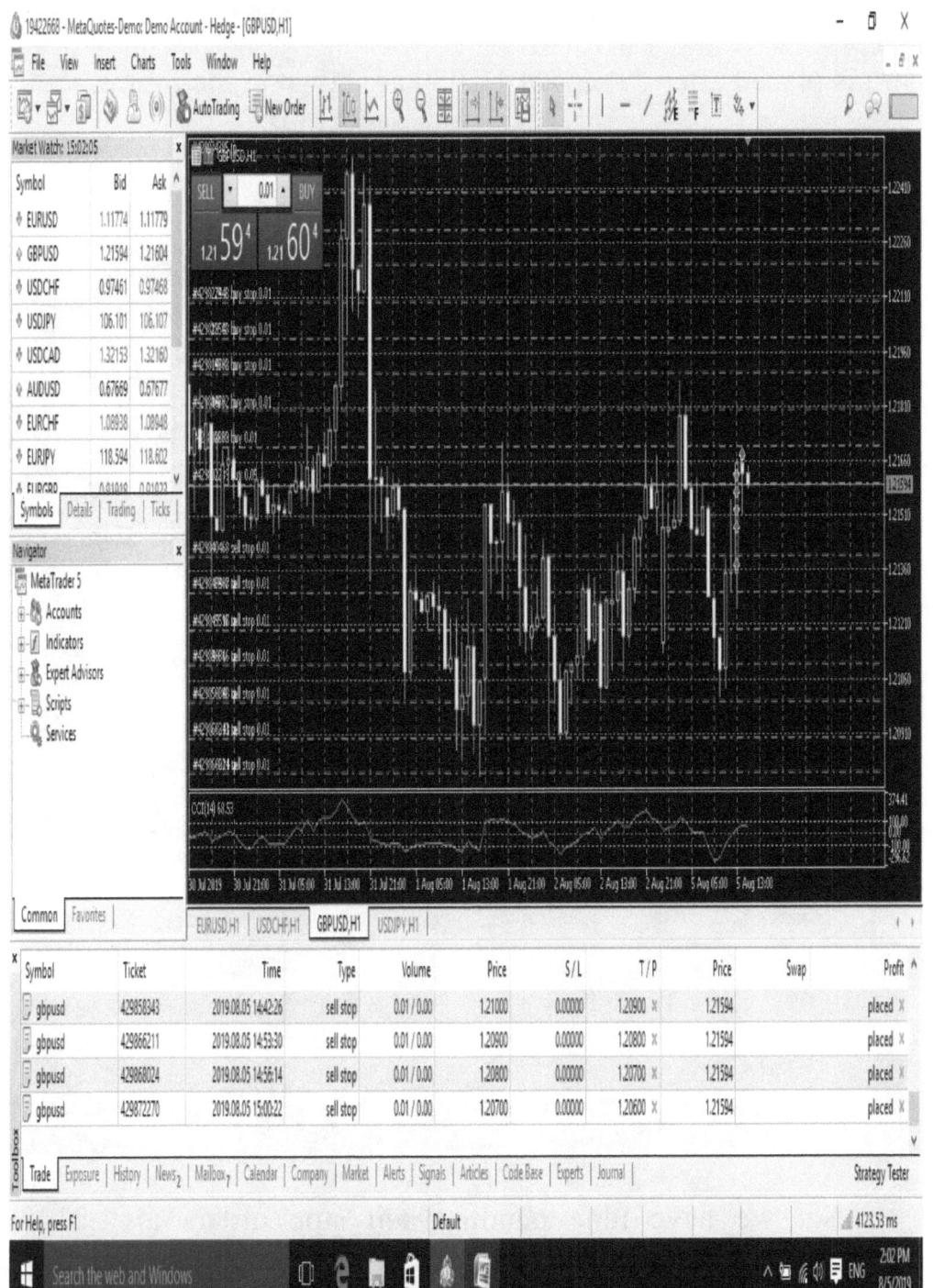

The ninth sell stop order is placed at 1.2060 and take profit limit is placed after 10 pips at 1.2050 as shown in the figure.

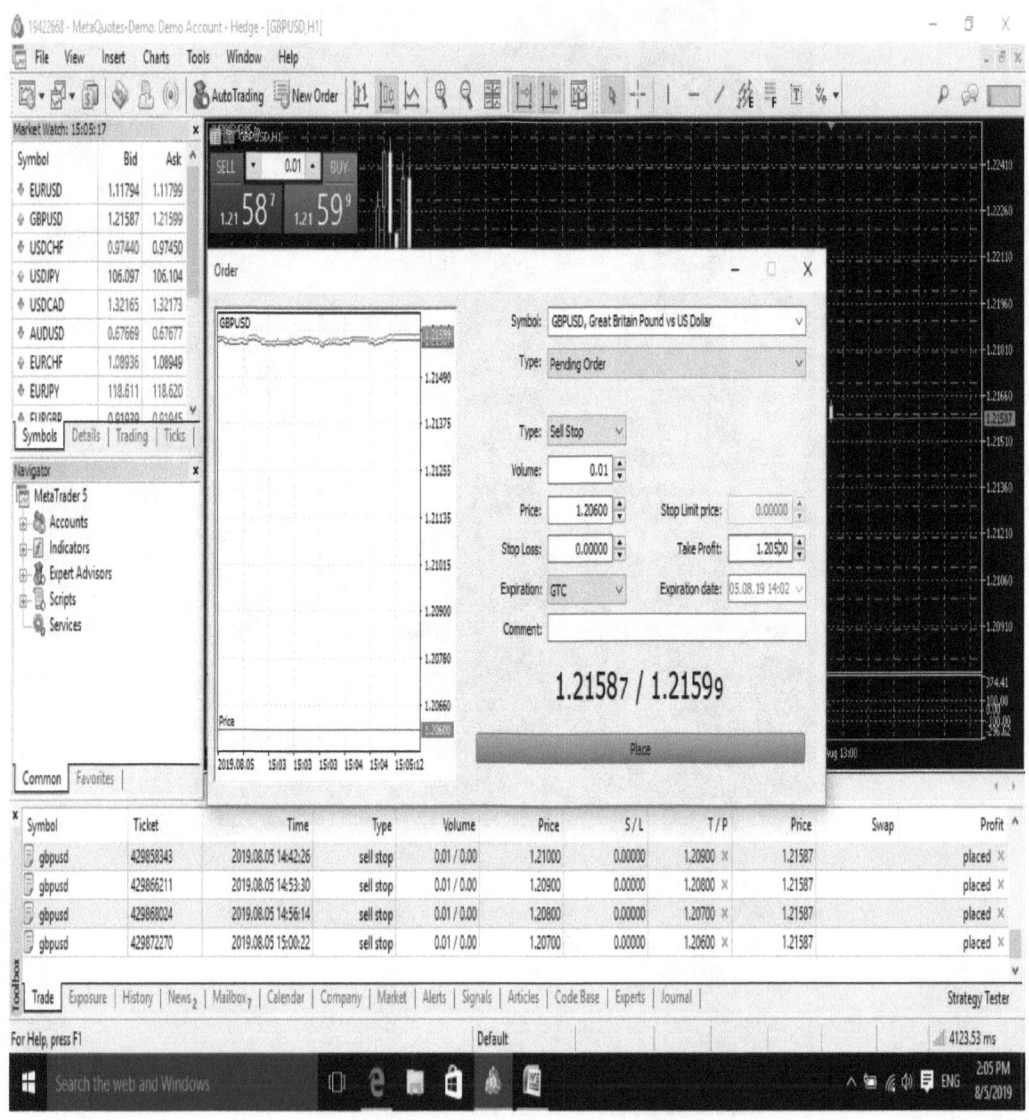

So, we have nine pending sell stop orders at 1.2140, 1.2130, 1.2120, 1,2110, 1.2100, 1.2090, 1.2080, 1.2070 and 1.2060 and nine profit taking limits at 1.2130, 1.2120, 1.2110, 1.2100, 1.2090, 1.2080, 1.2070, 1.2060 and 1.2050 respectively.

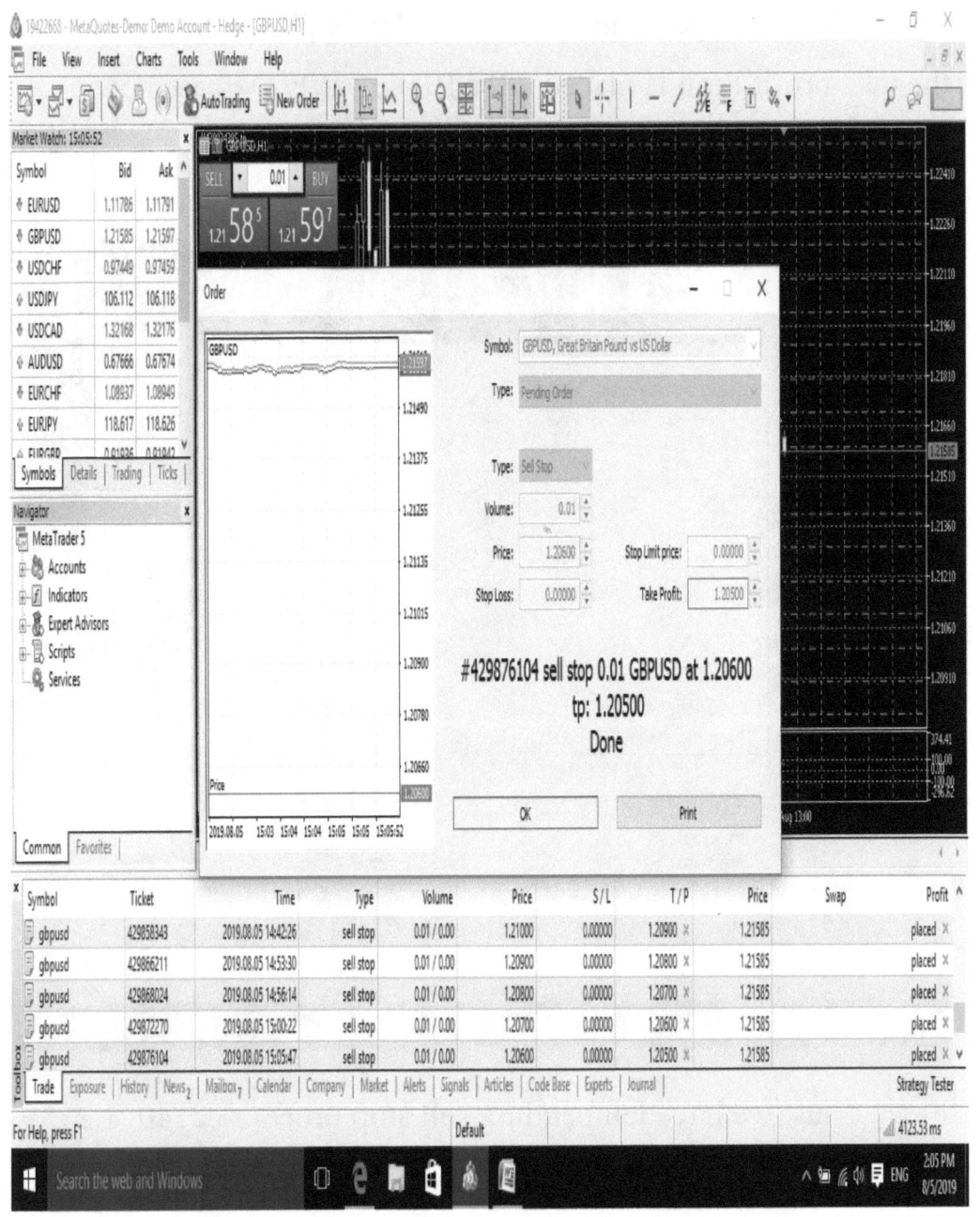

The tenth pending sell stop order is placed at 1.2050 and the take profit limit is placed after 10 pips at 1.2040 as shown.

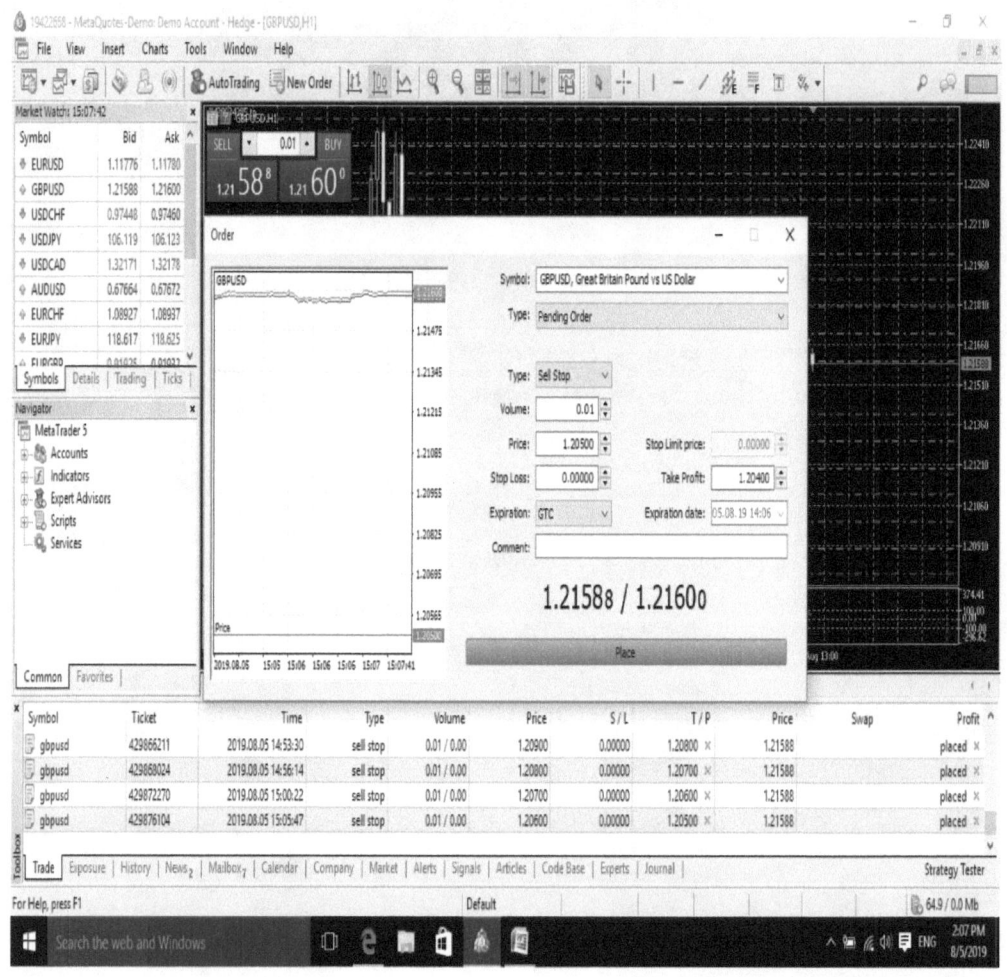

Thus, we have ten pending sell stop orders: 1.2140, 1.2130, 1.2120, 1,2110, 1.2100, 1.2090, 1.2080, 1.2080, 1.2070, 1.2060 and 1.2050 and ten profit taking limits at 1.2130, 1.2120, 1.2110, 1. 2100, 1.2090, 1.2080, 1.2070, 1.2060, 1.2050 and 1.2040 respectively.

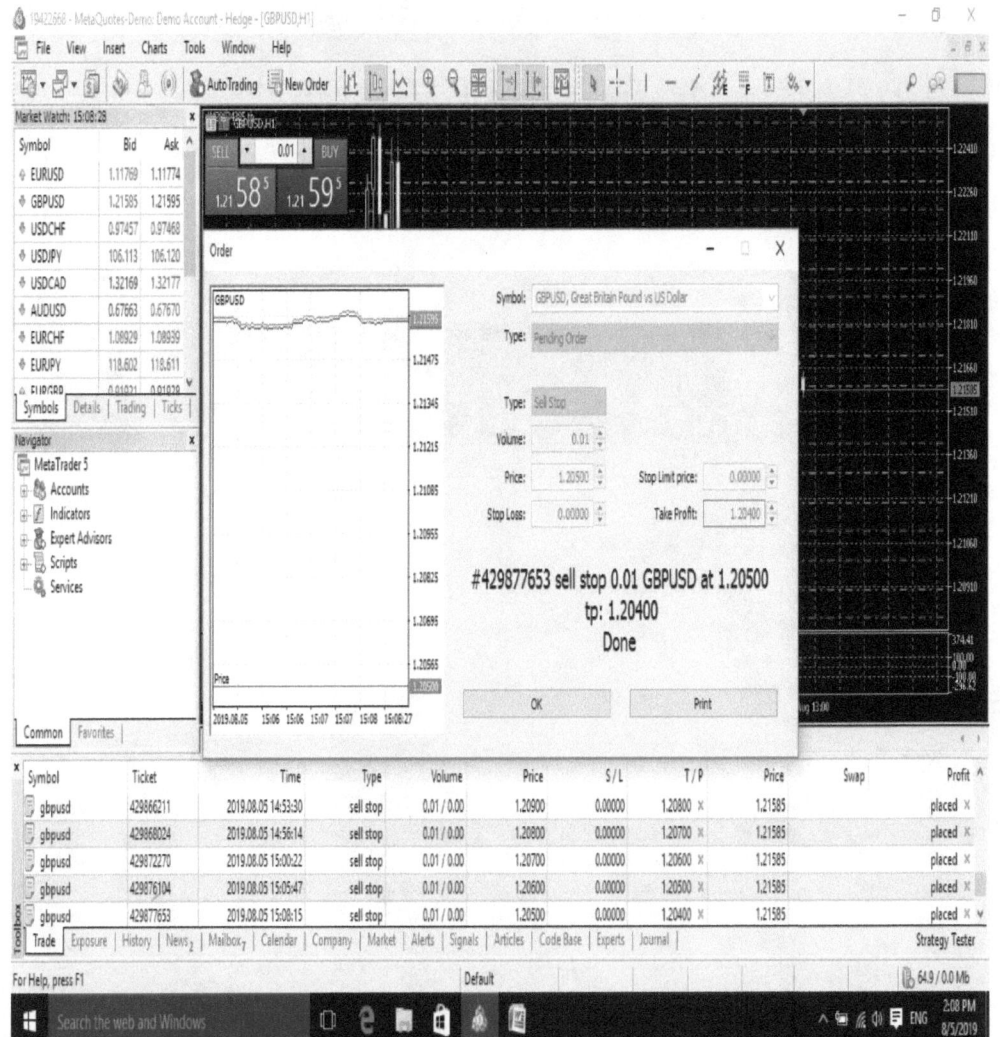

Now we have two groups, the first group consists of ten buy stop orders and ten profit-taking limits and the second group consists of ten sell stop orders and ten profit-taking limits.

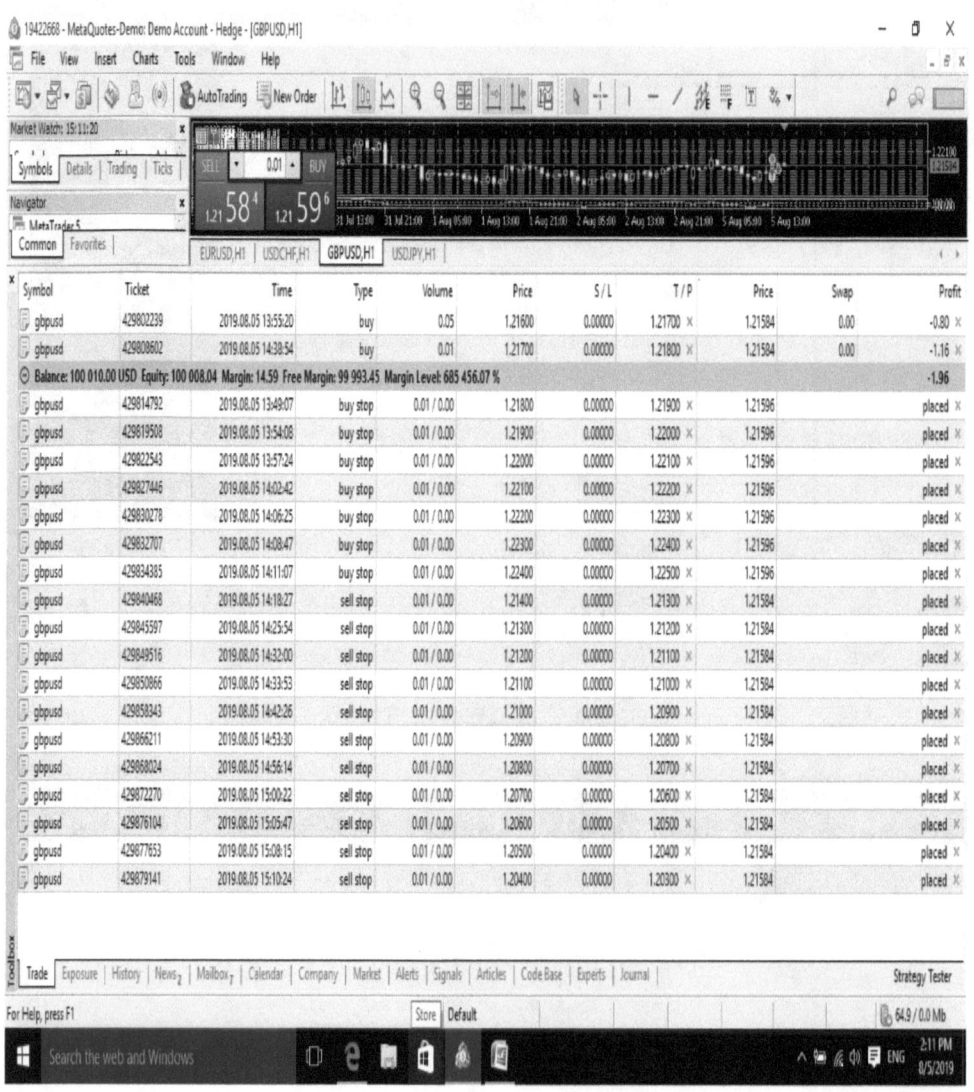

The number of pending orders can be increased to 15 or 20 pending buy stop and sell stop orders.

Taking Profits

As we can see in the following figure, two buy and take profit orders were executed.

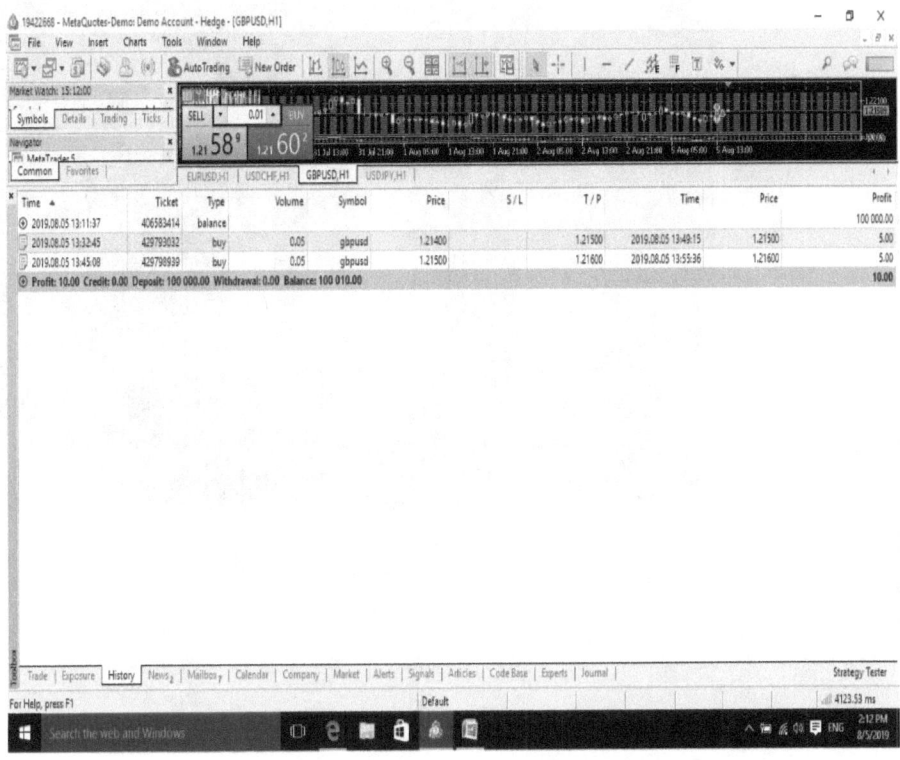

As we can see in the following figure, another buy order has been executed and profit taking. So, three buy orders were executed and closed at profit taking limits.

As we see the position after making profits.

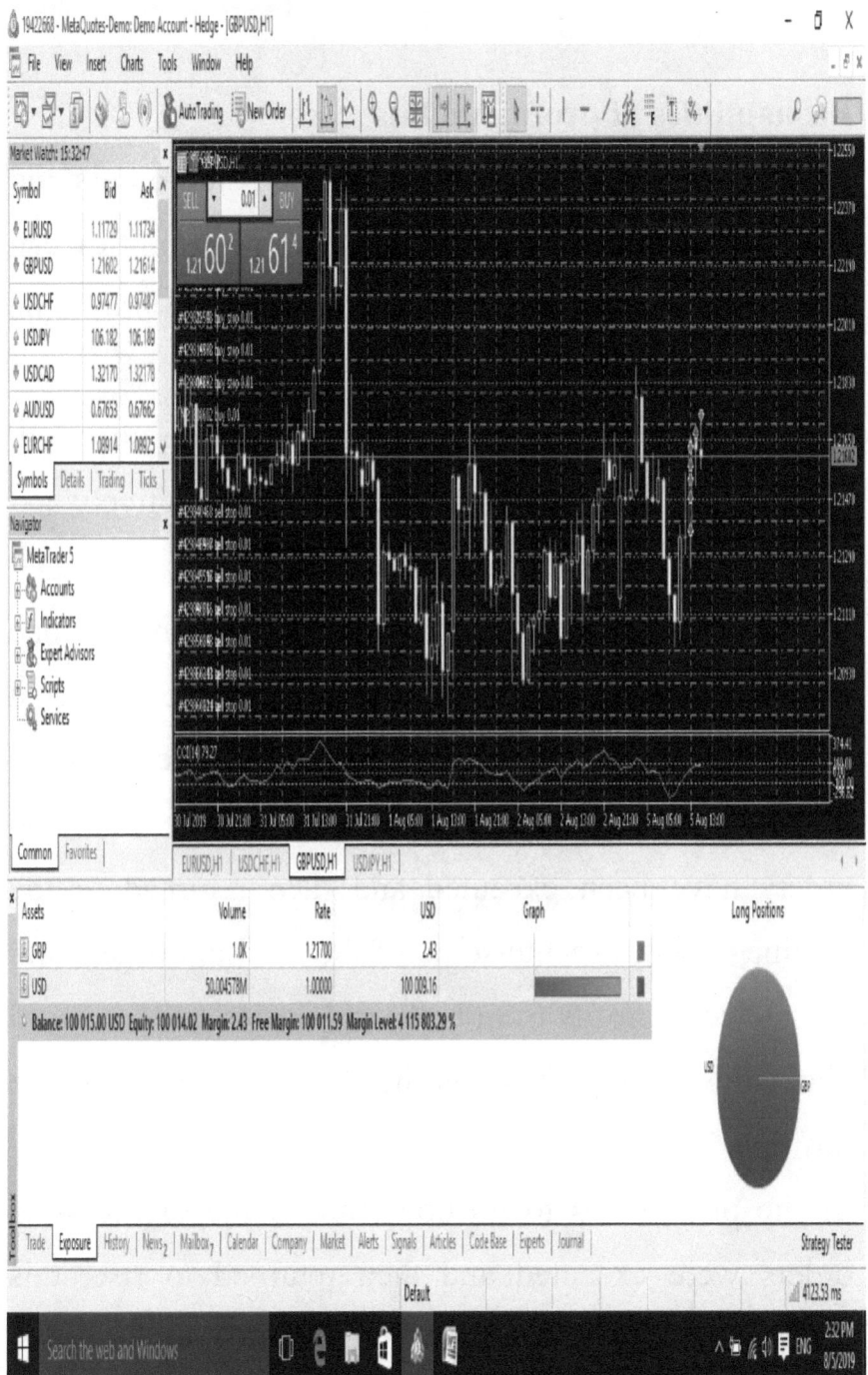

Probabilities of profit and loss

1- After placing a set of buy stop and sell stop orders and determining profit limits, a range of probabilities can occur and mostly leads to the creation of profitable positions.

2- If the price tends to go up, i.e. going in one direction, pending buy stop orders are executed consecutively and therefore all profit limits are met.

3- If the price tends to go down, i.e. moving in one direction, the pending sell stop orders are executed consecutively and therefore all profit limits are realized.

4- If the price tends to rise and some of the buy stop orders have been executed and then returned to the decline, it will execute some of the sell stop orders and thus achieve profits from both, and orders can be closed manually at any time as needed at any profitable position.

5- If the price tends to go down and some of the sales orders were executed and then returned to rise, this leads to making profits from the both orders and can be closed manually at any time as needed at any profitable position.

6- When a buy stop order is executed and the price starts to go up and then suddenly it starts falling before it reaches the profit-taking level, the execution of the sell orders begins but at the same time the buy order continues to lose, this may be compensated by the return of the trend to climb again.

7- So, we have four cases of profit versus one case of an uncertain loss, i.e. the probability of profit is 80% and the probability of loss is 20%.

The Second Strategy
(Instant Execution Orders)

The second proposed strategy is to place a set of instant buy and sell orders with gradual upward take profit limits.

The first Ten Orders

The first instant order, a buy order, is placed for the EURUSD, as an example, at the current price of 1.1179 and taking profit after almost 10 pips at 1.1190 or more.

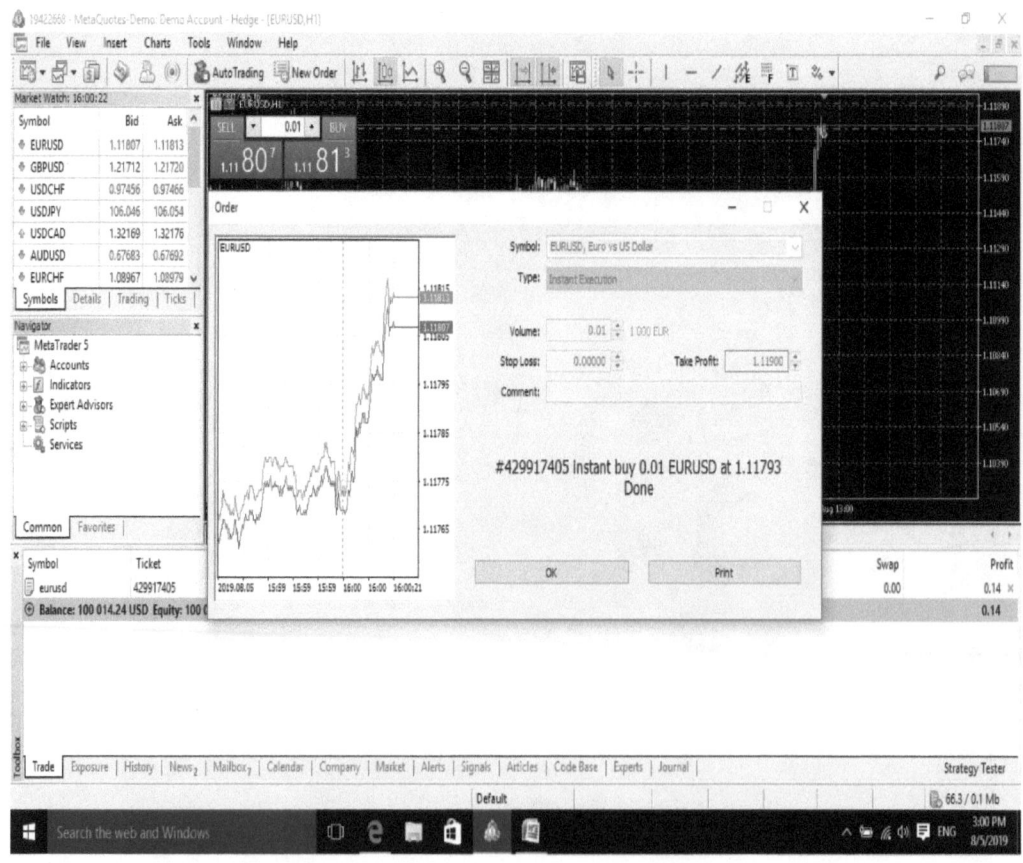

The second instant execution order is a sell order placed for the EURUSD at the current price of 1.1176 and take profit after 10 pips at 1.1160 or more.

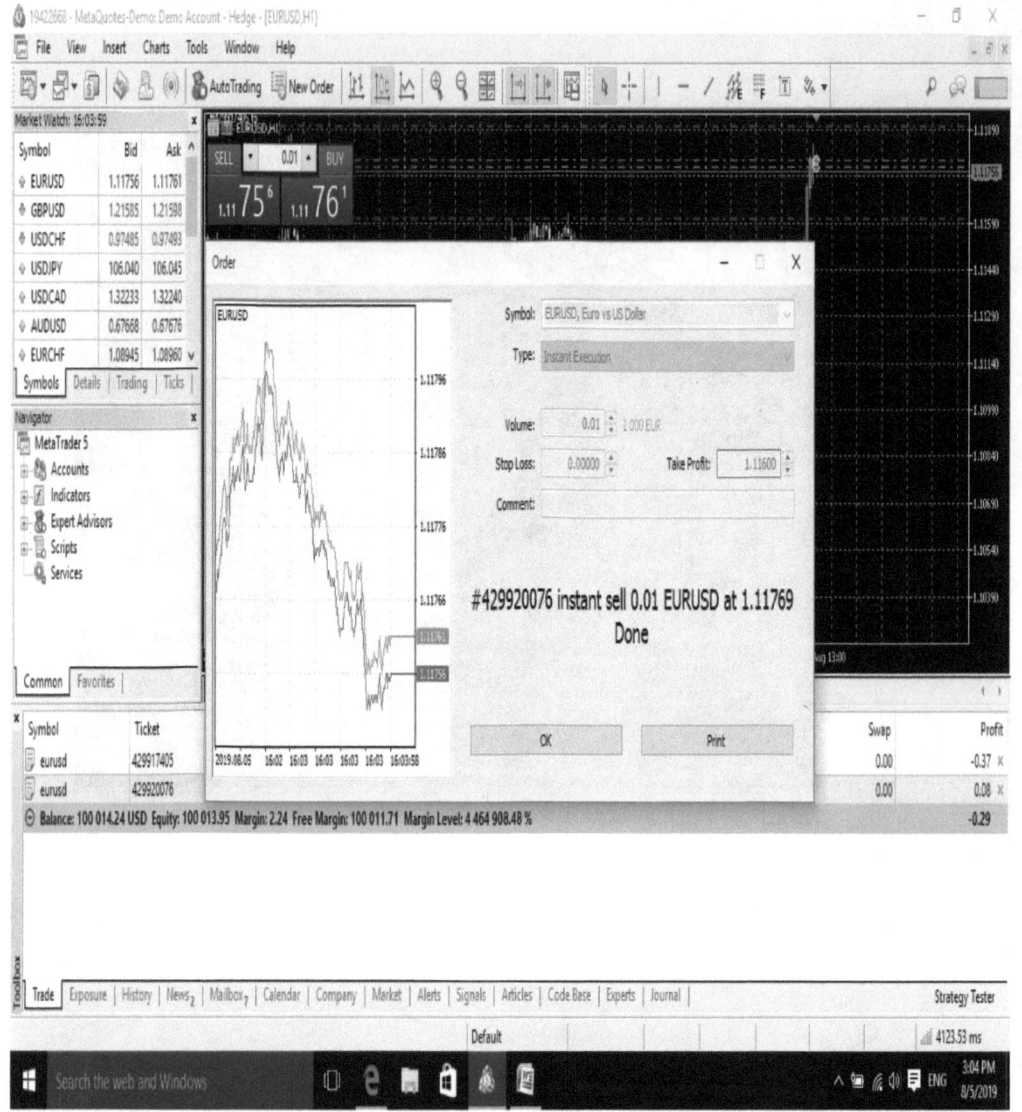

We note that the buy order is followed by a sell order, and so on until the group is completed, unlike the pending orders strategy, where a set of buy orders can be placed in batch and then sales orders.

Now we have two instant orders, a buy order and a sell order plus two profit-taking limits, both after 10 pips.

The third order is a buy order placed at the current price of 1.1175 and a take profit after 25 pips at 1.1200.

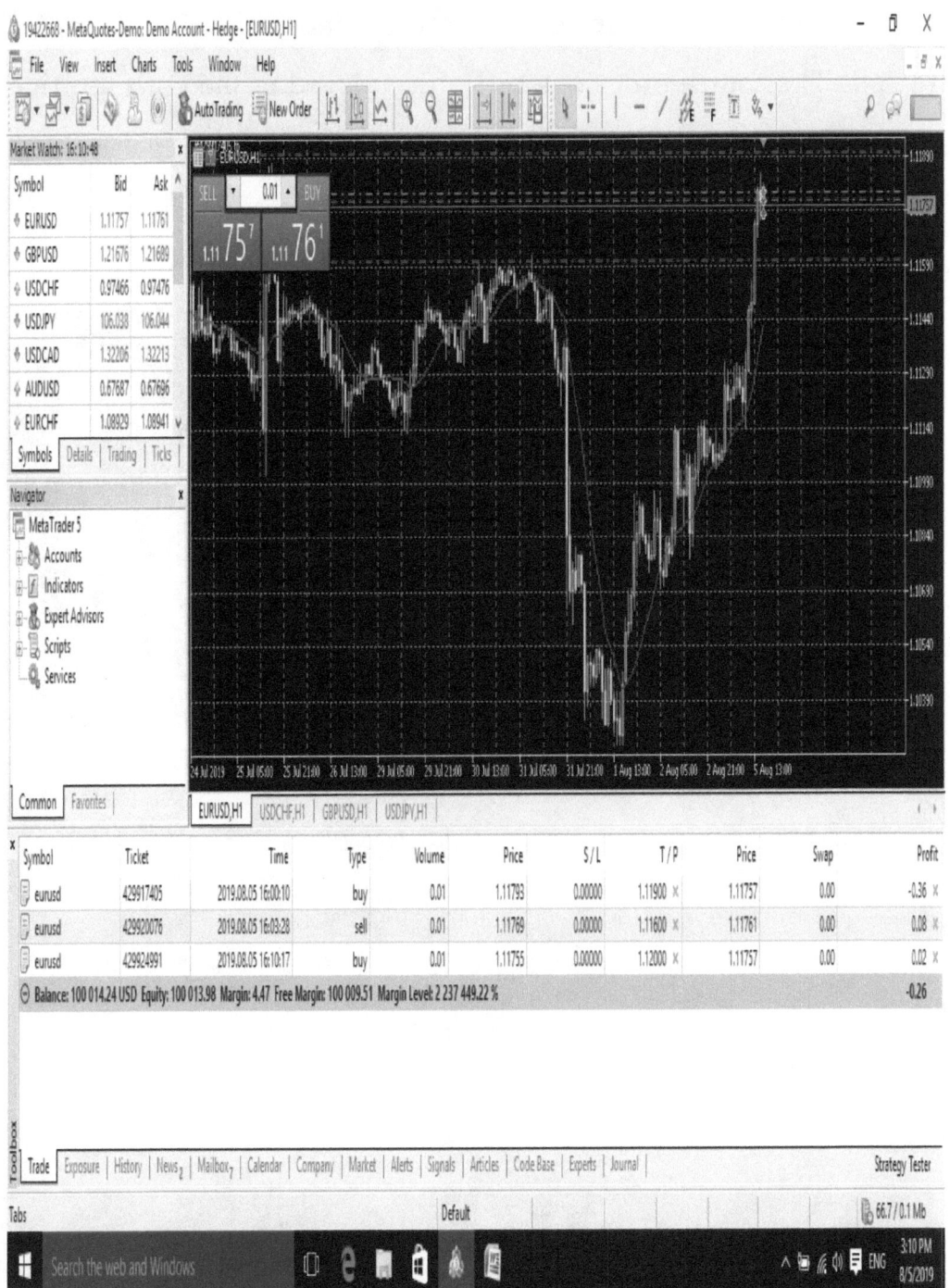

Now we have three orders, two orders to buy and one order to sell. The fourth order is a sell order placed at the current price of 1.1174 and a take profit after 25 pips at 1.1150.

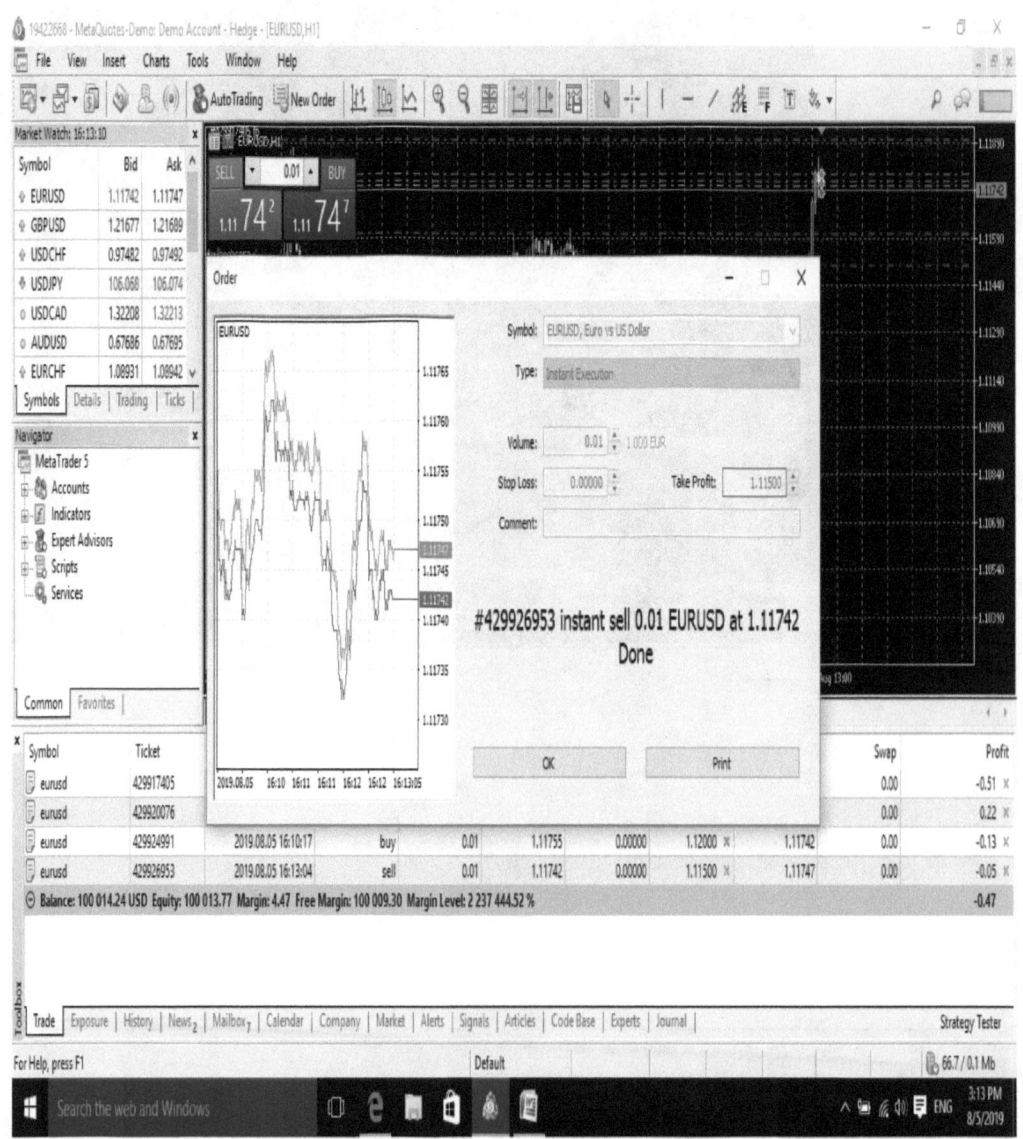

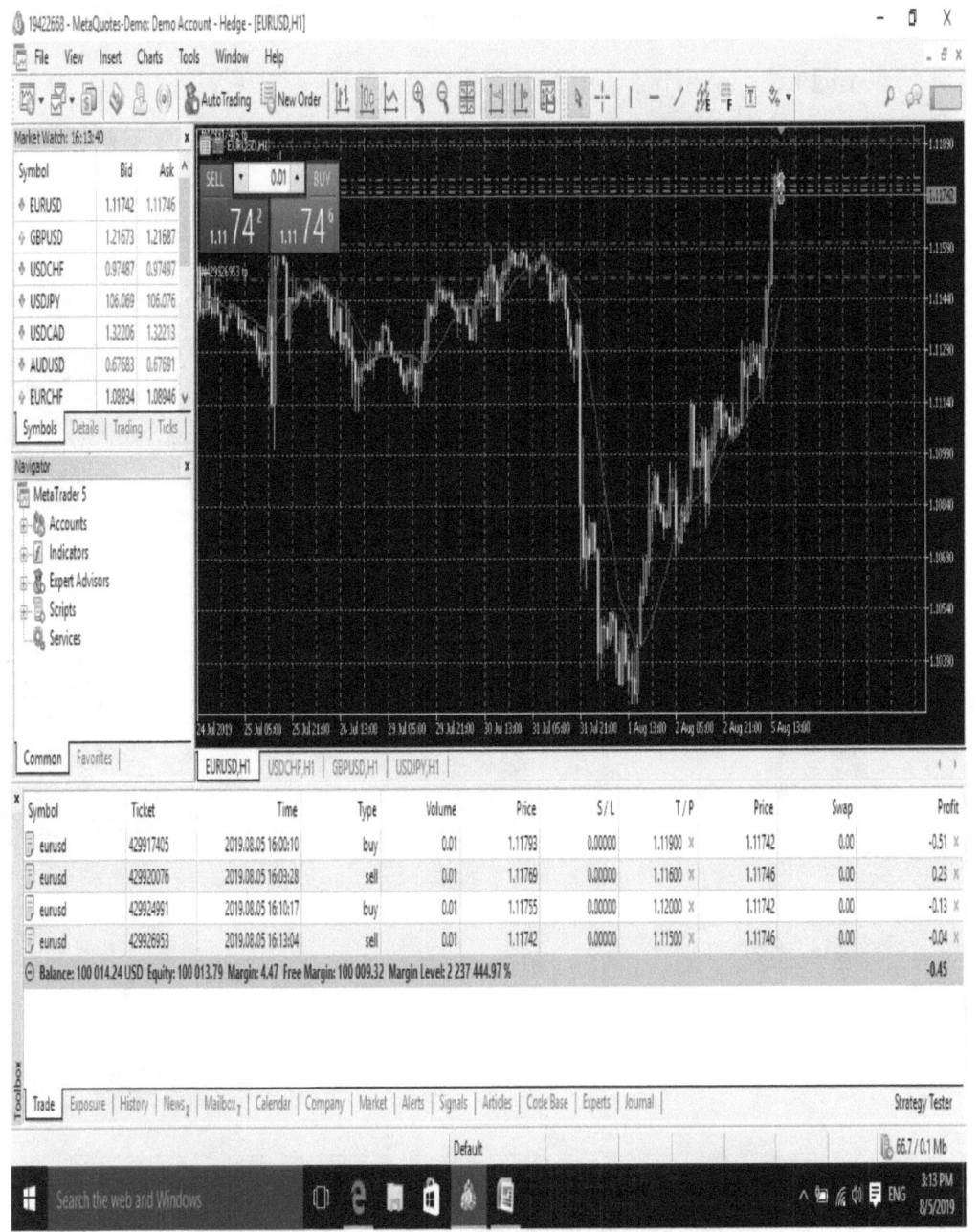

Now we have four orders, two for buy, two for sell and four take profit limits.

The fifth order is a buy order placed at the current price of 1.1175 and take profit after 35 pips at 1.1210.

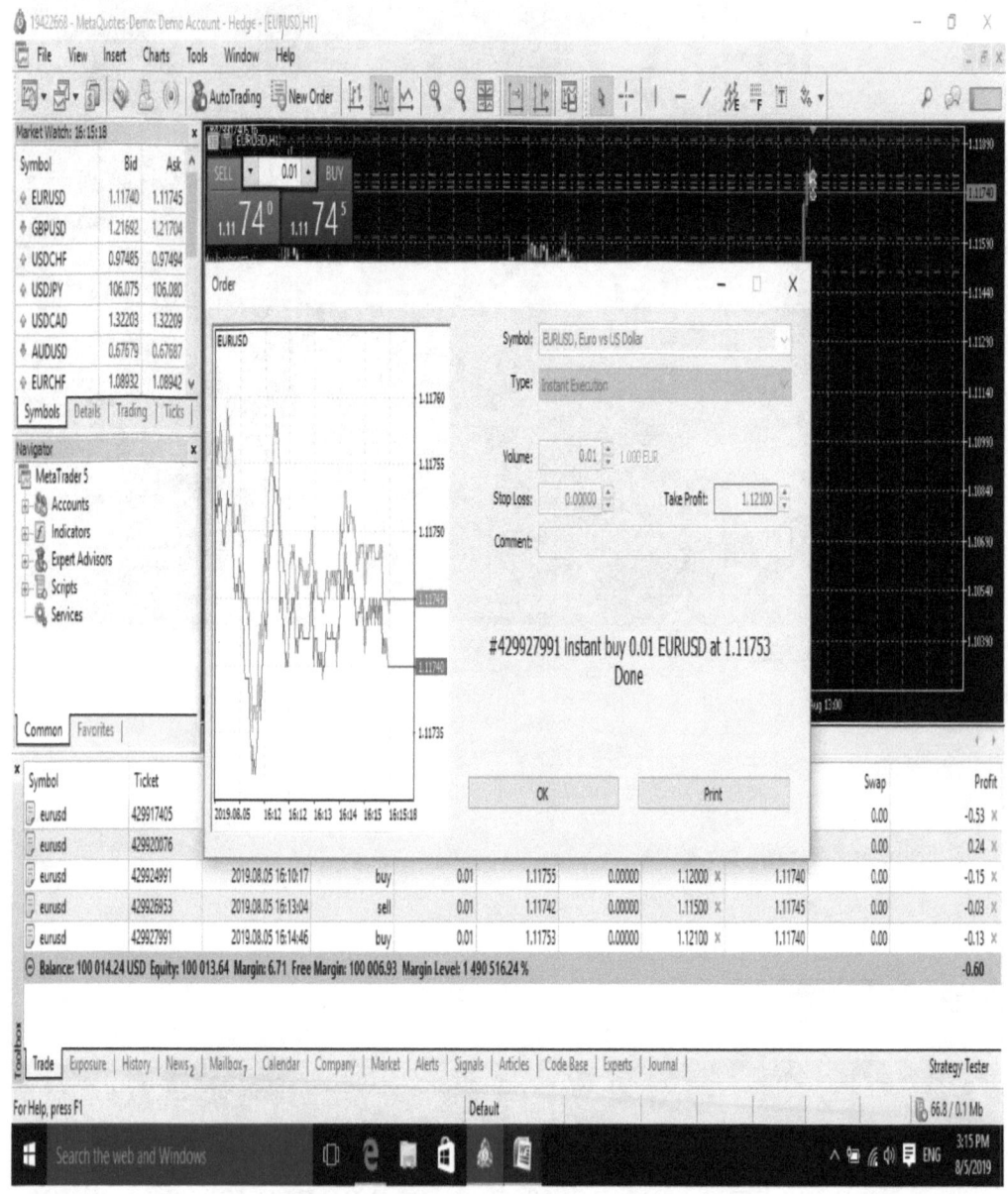

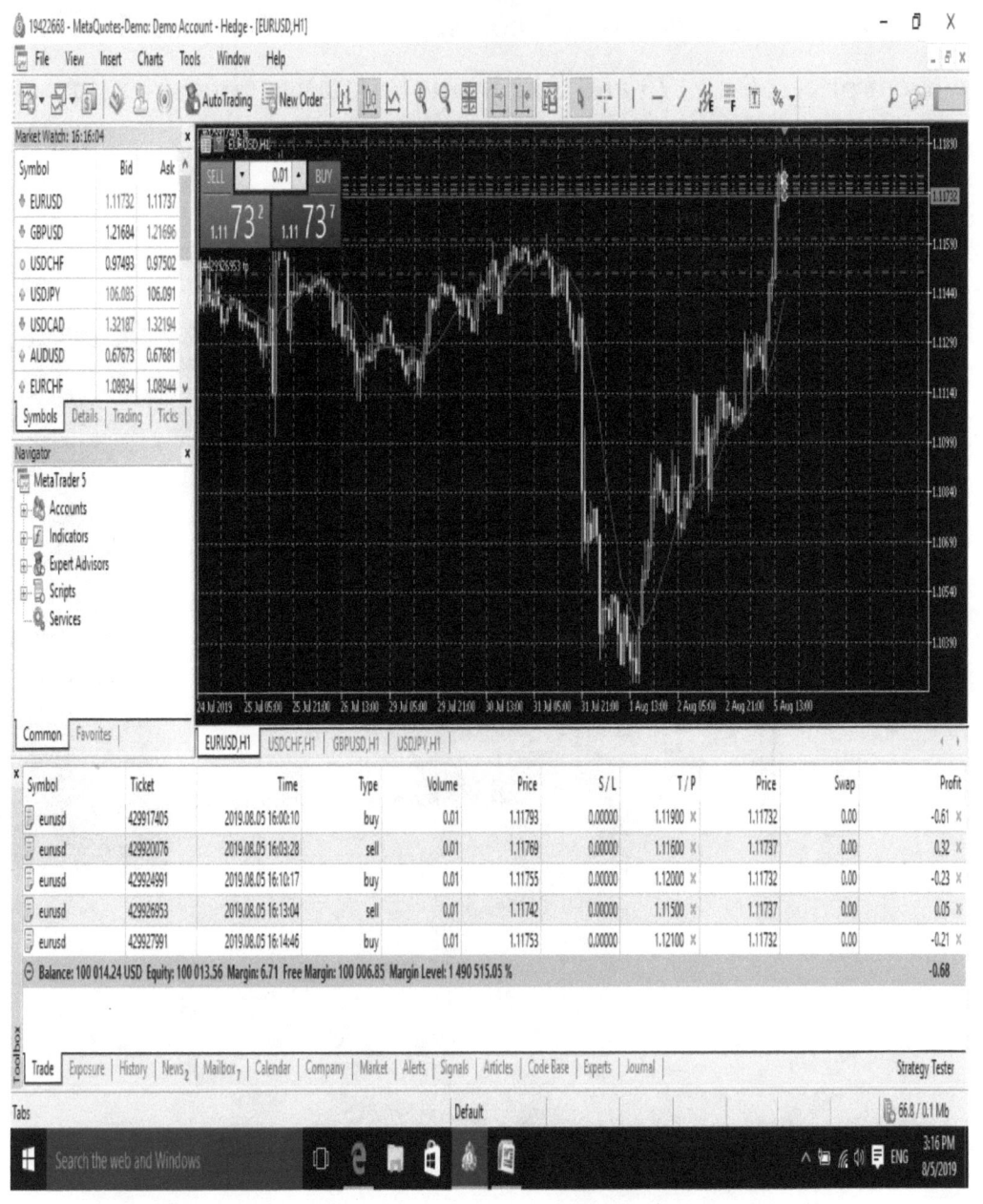

Now we have five orders three to buy and two to sell.

The sixth order is, of course, a sell order placed at the current price of 1.1173 and take profit limit after almost 35 pips at 1.1140.

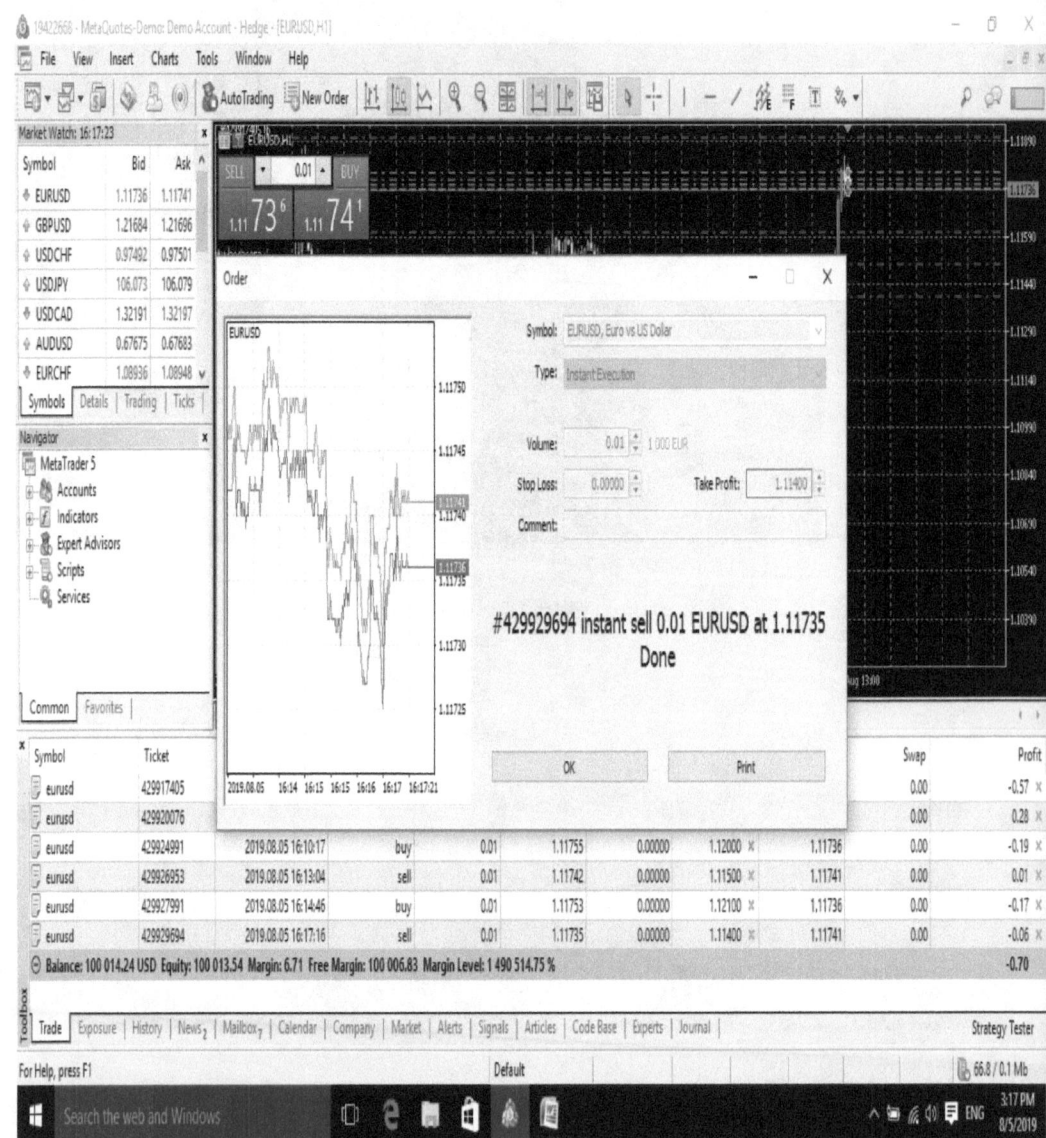

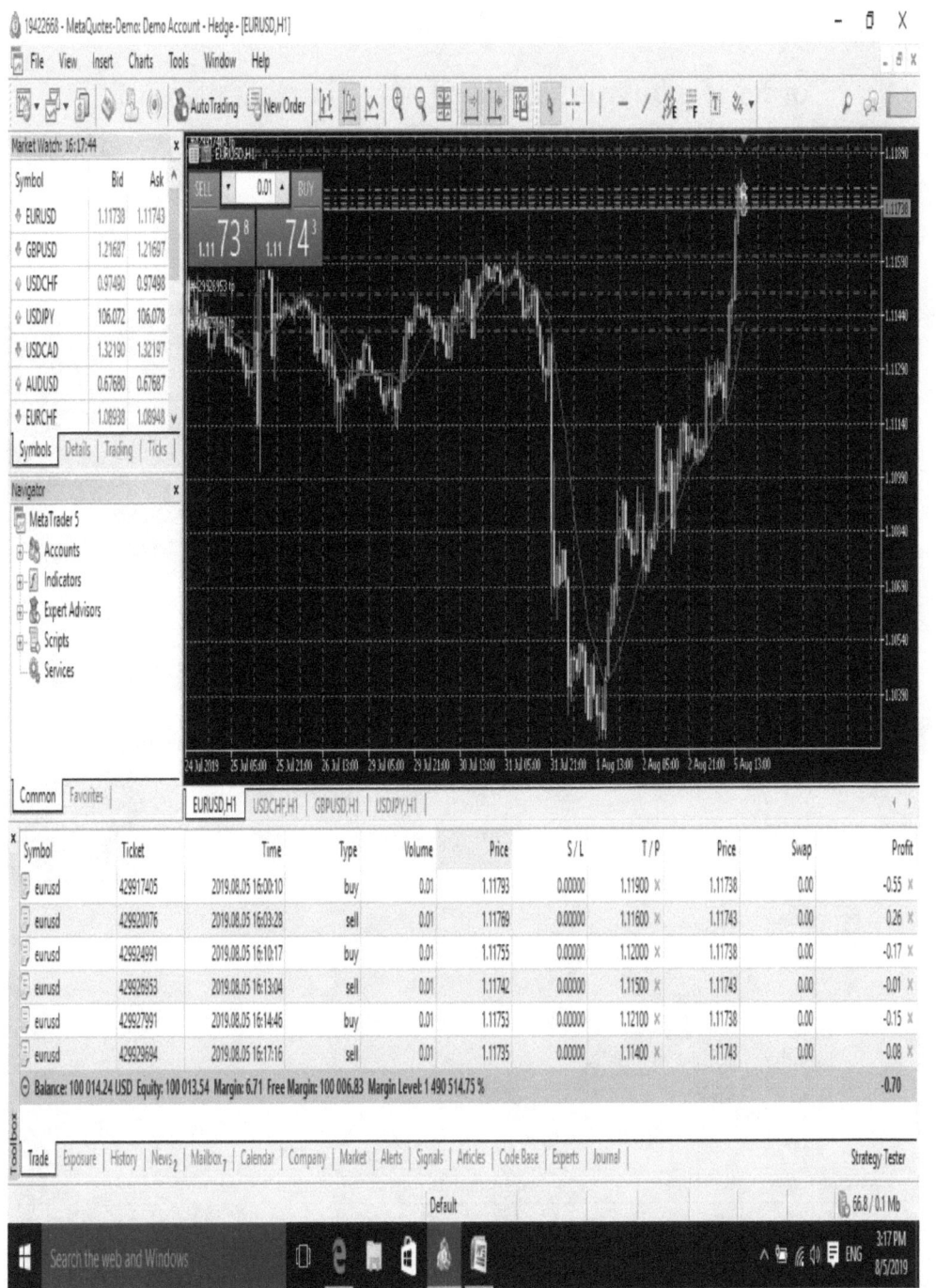

Now we have six orders, three orders to buy and three orders to sell.

The 7th order is a buy order placed at the current price of 1.1172 and take profit after 45 pips at 1.1220.

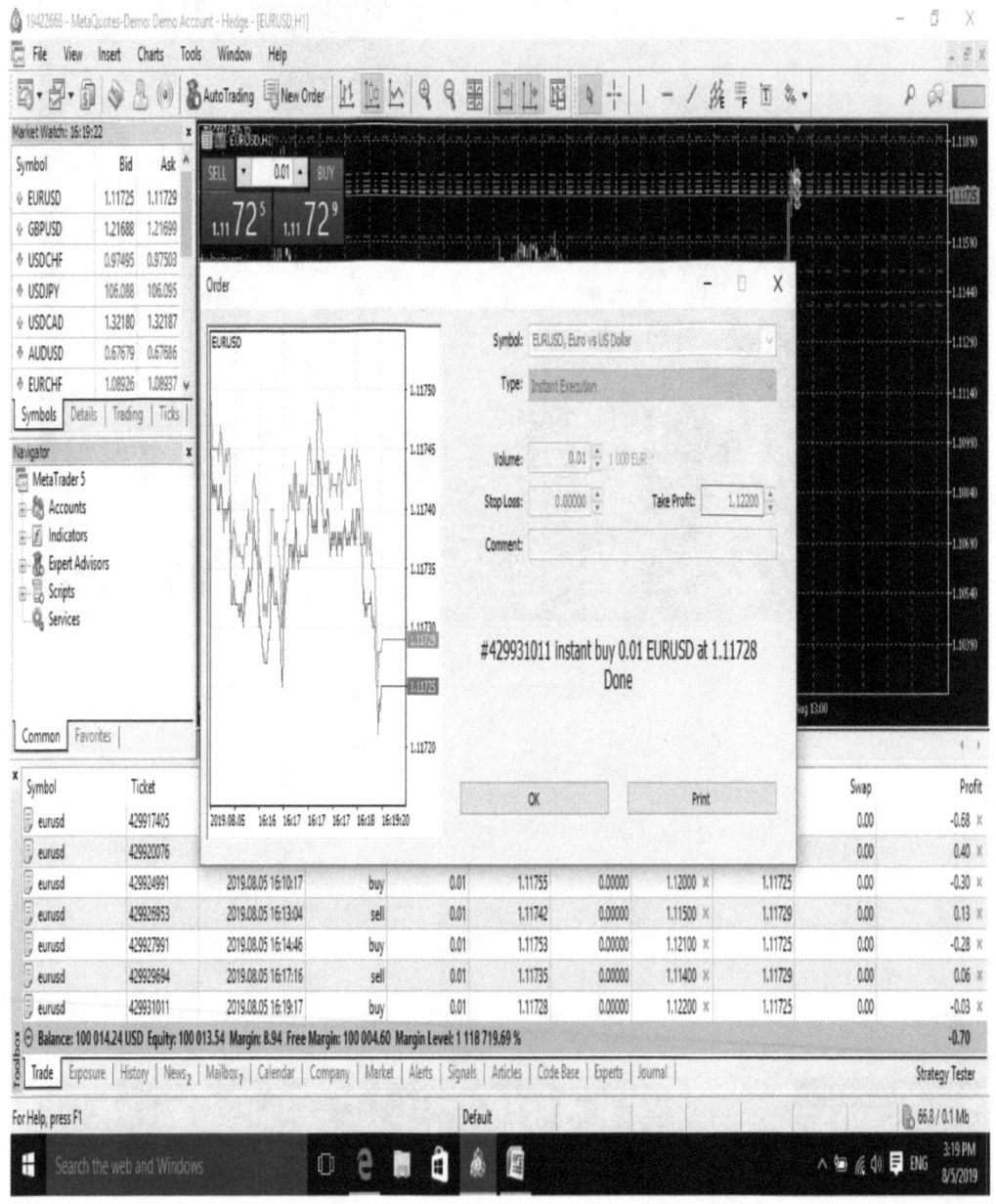

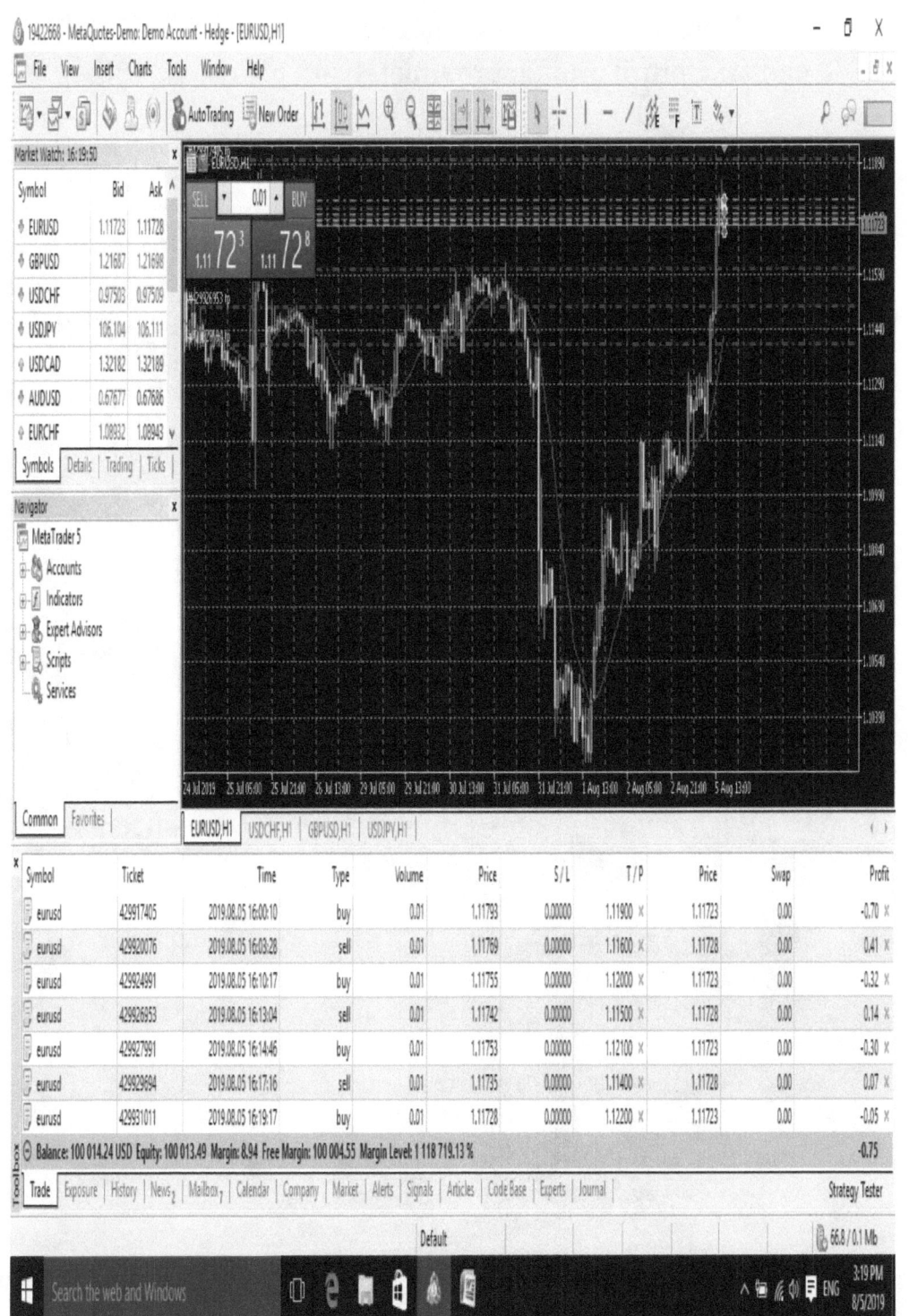

Now we have seven orders, four to buy and three to sell.

The 8th order is a sell order placed at the current price of 1.1172 and take profit after approximately 45 pips at 1.1130.

Now we have eight orders, four buy orders and four sell orders.

The 9th order is a buy order placed at the current price of 1.1173 and take profit after almost 55 pips at 1.1230.

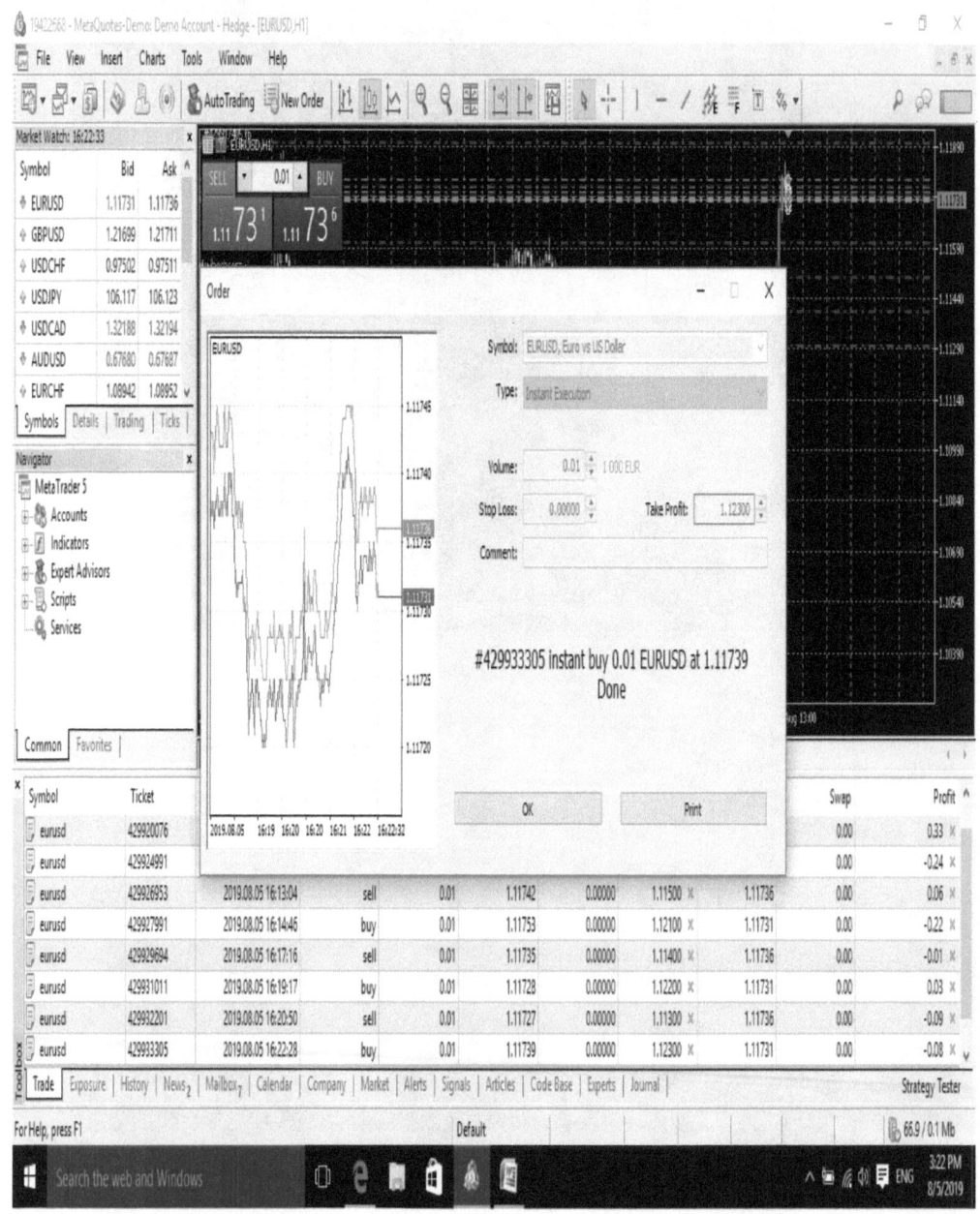

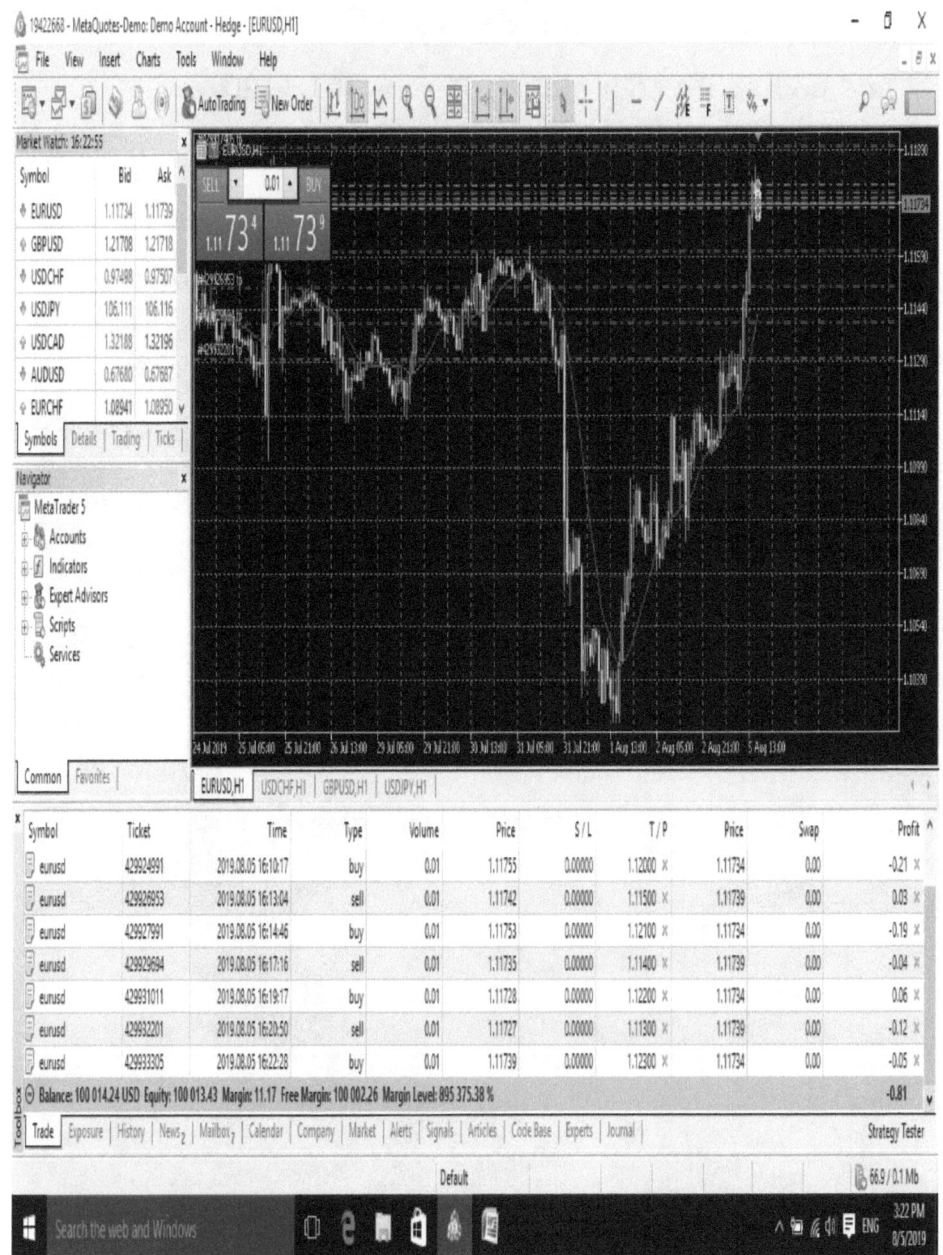

Now we have nine orders, five of them for buy and four for sell.

The 10th order is a sell order placed at the current price of 1.1173 and take profit after almost 55 pips at 1.1120.

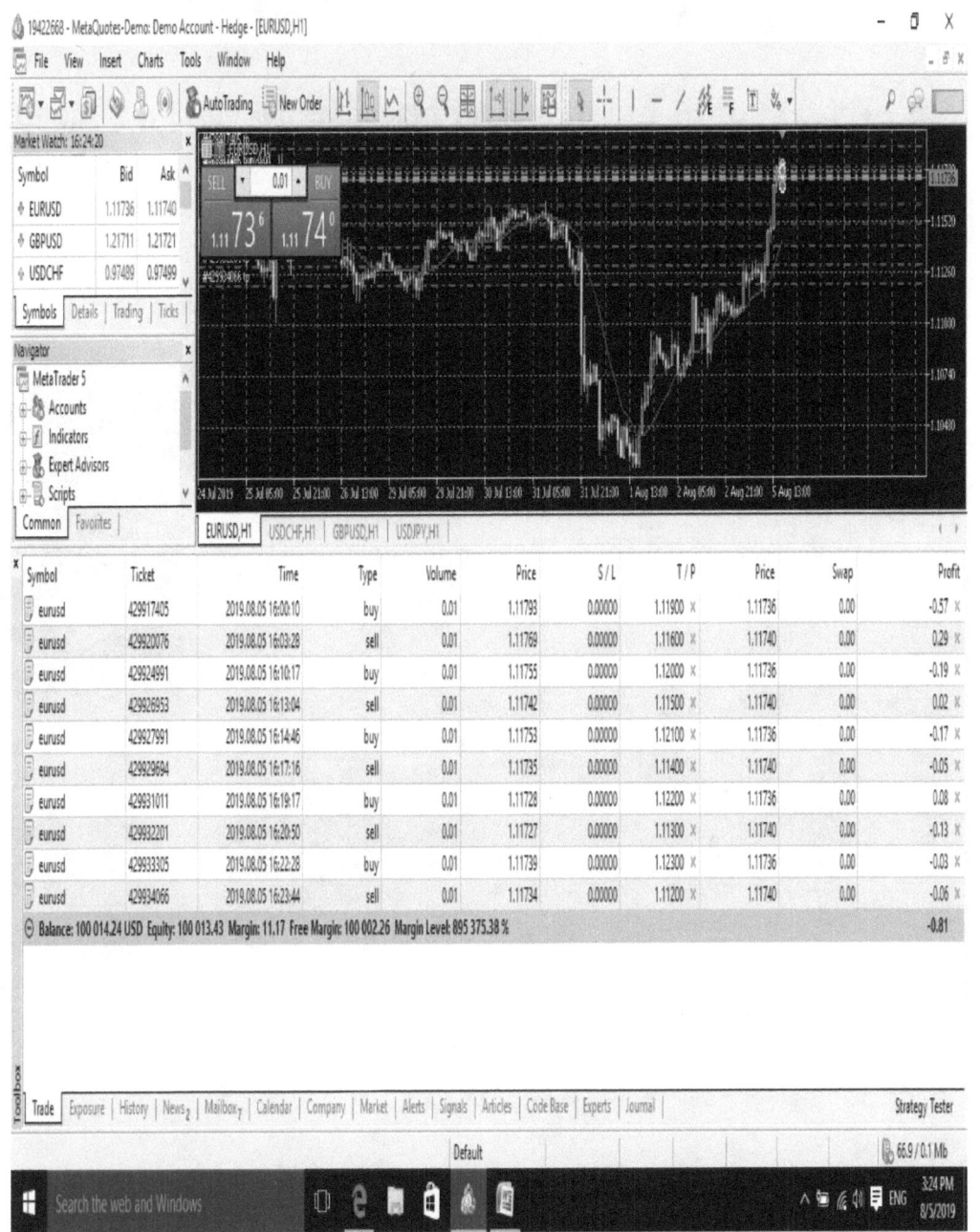

Now we have ten orders, five of them for buy and five for sell.

The Second Ten Orders

The 11th order is a buy order placed at the current price of 1.1174 and take profit after 65 pips at 1.1280.

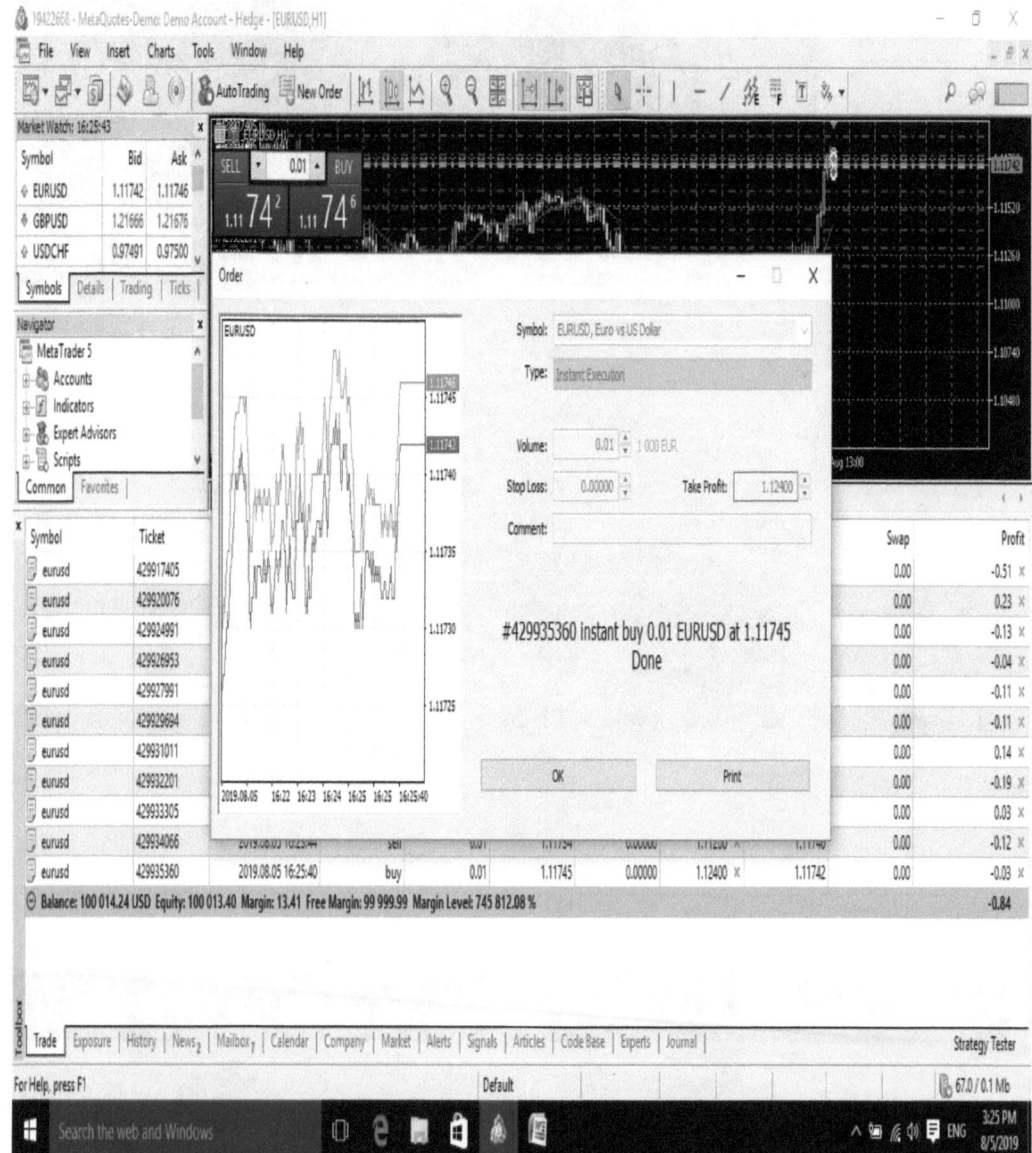

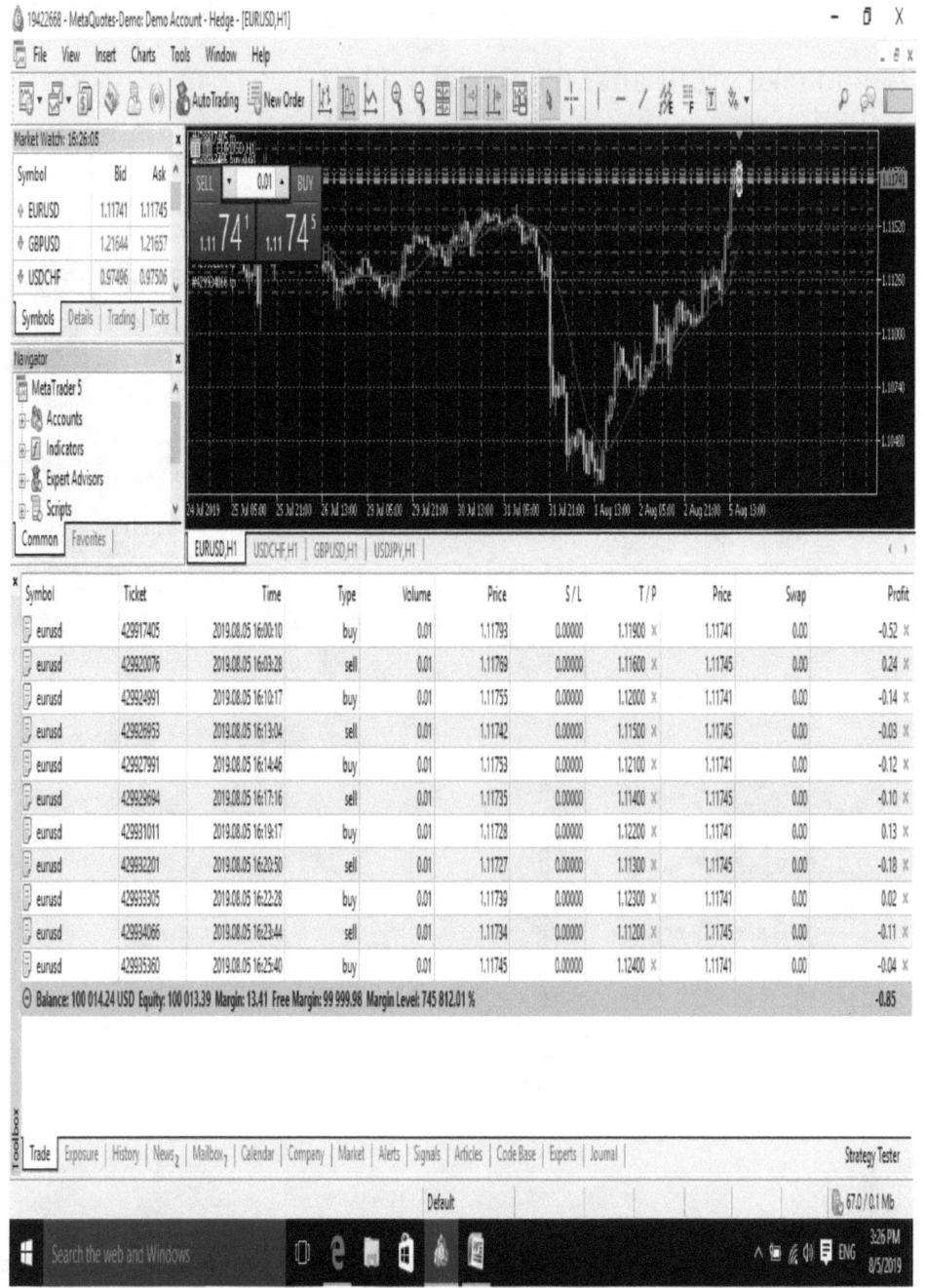

Now we have eleven orders, six to buy and five to sell.

The 12th order is a sell order placed at the current price of 1.1175 and take profit after 65 pips at 1.1110.

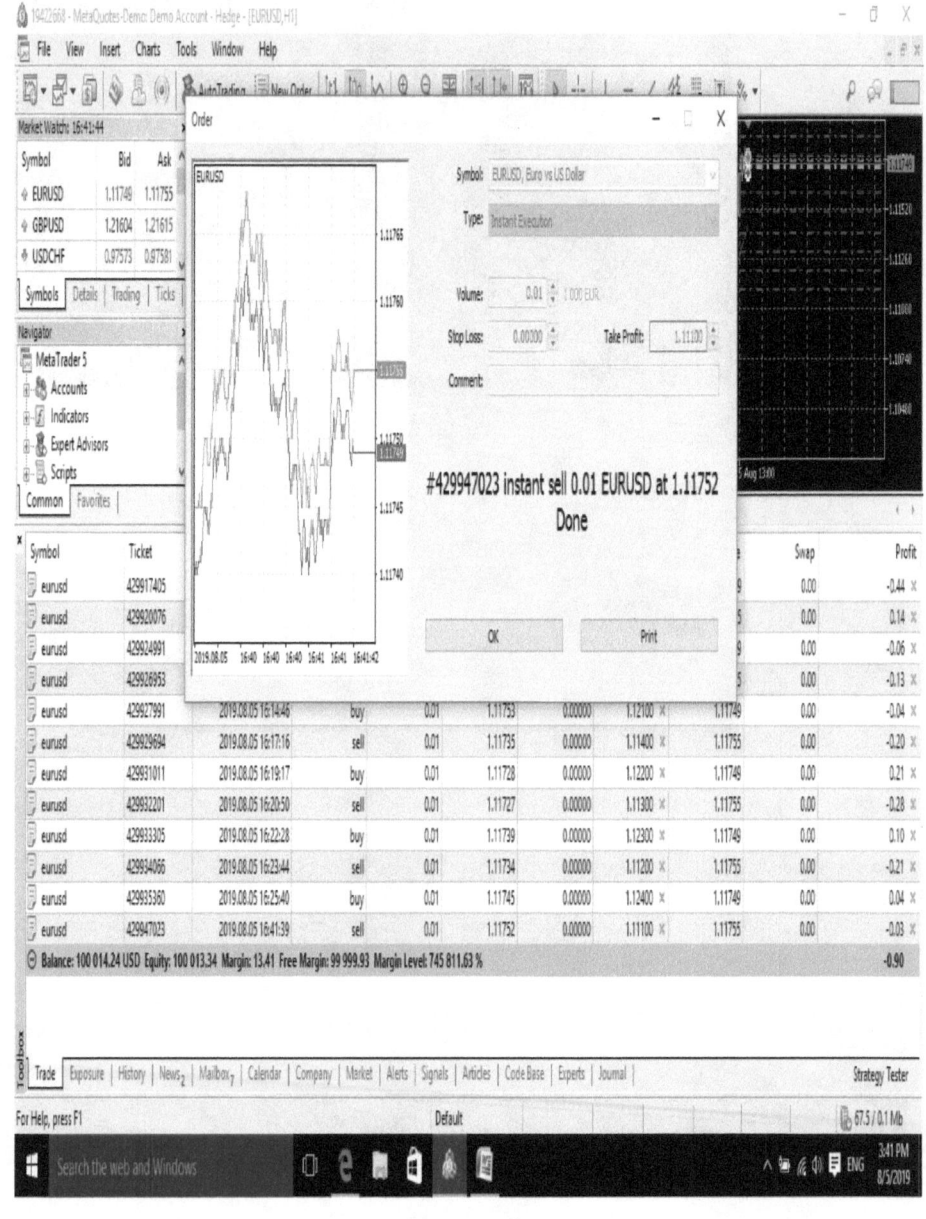

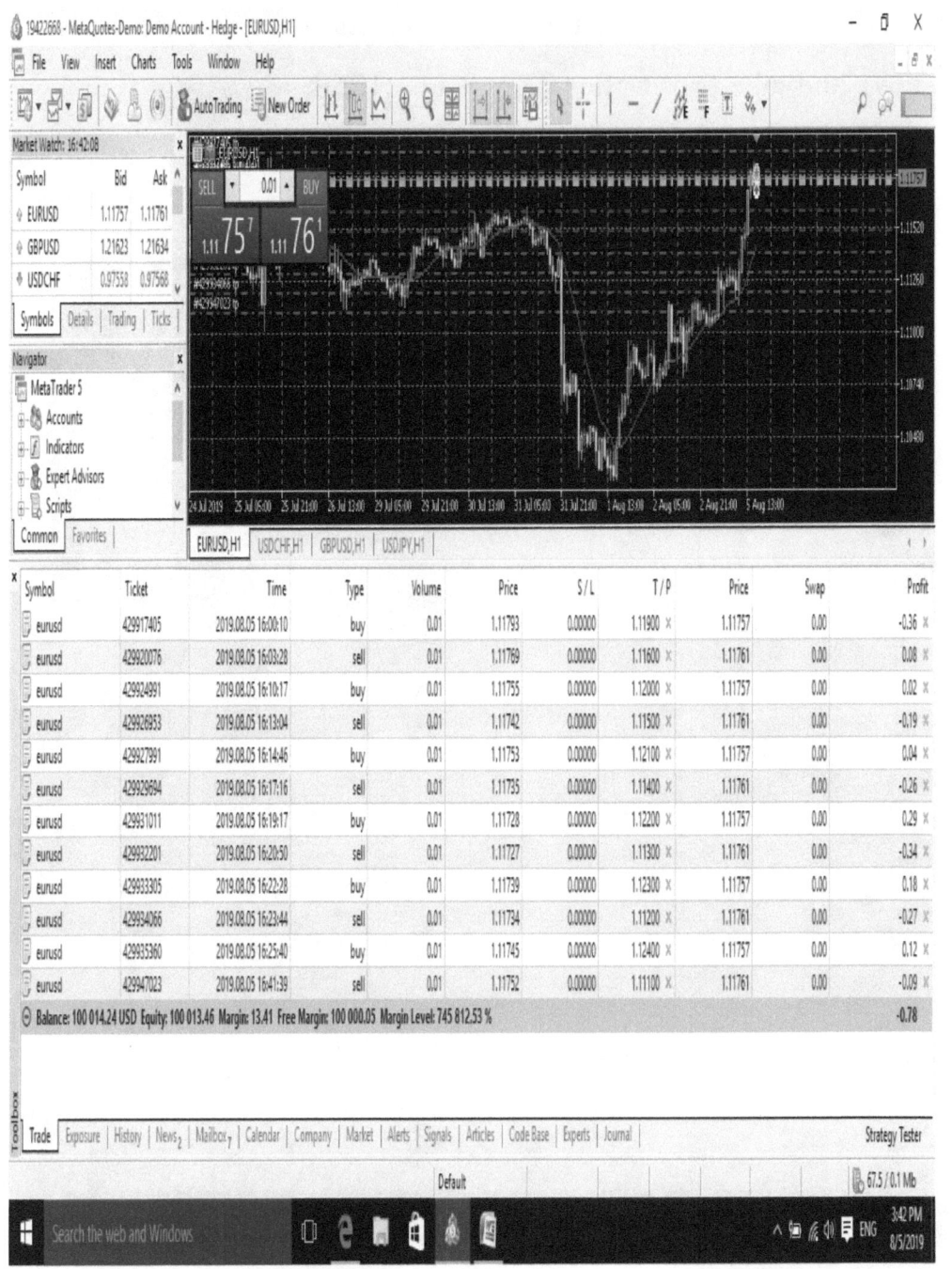

Now we have twelve orders, six to buy and six to sell.

The 13th order is a buy order placed at the current price of 1.1181 and take profit after 70 pips at 1.1250.

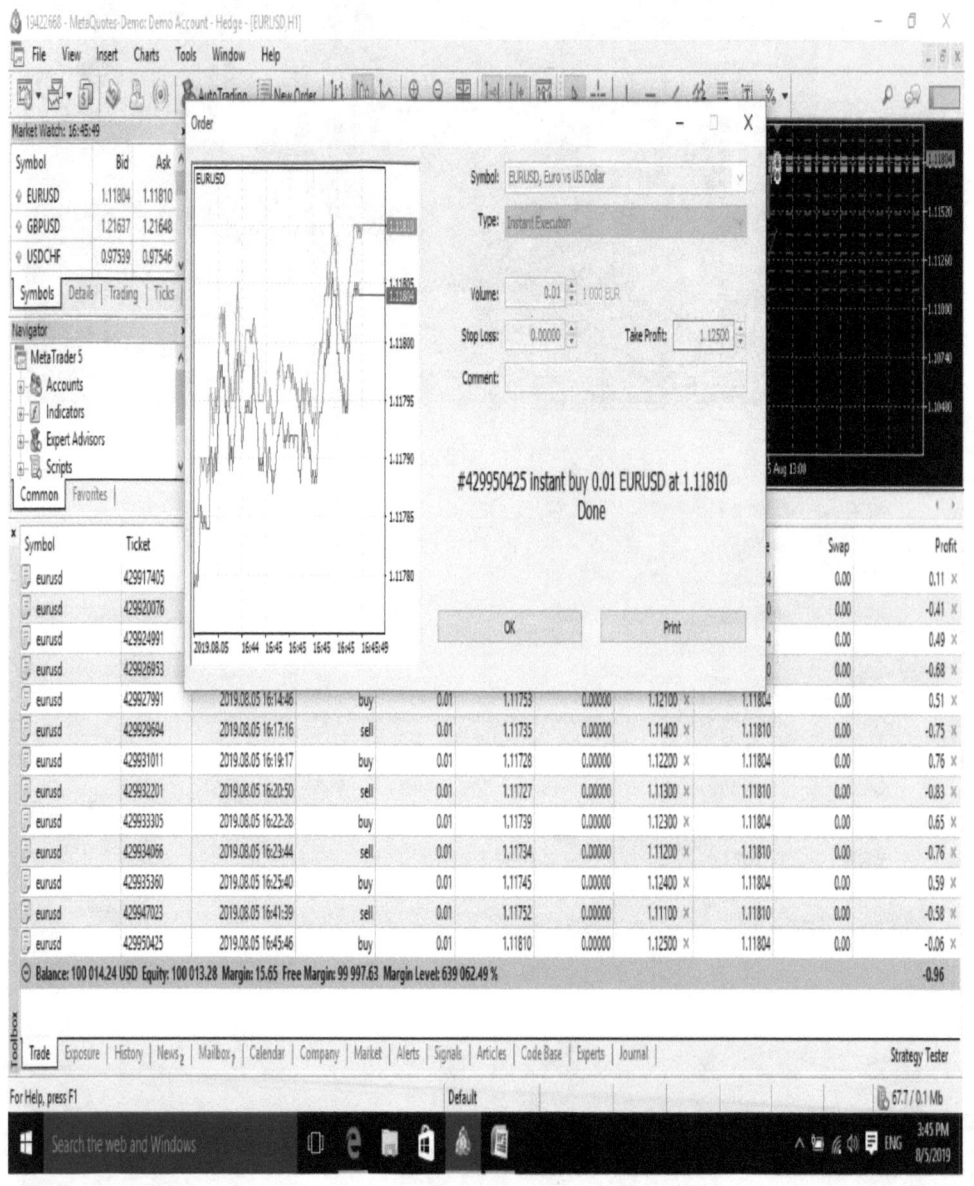

The 14th order is a sell order placed at the current price of 1.1182 and a take profit limit of approximately 80 pips at 1.1100.

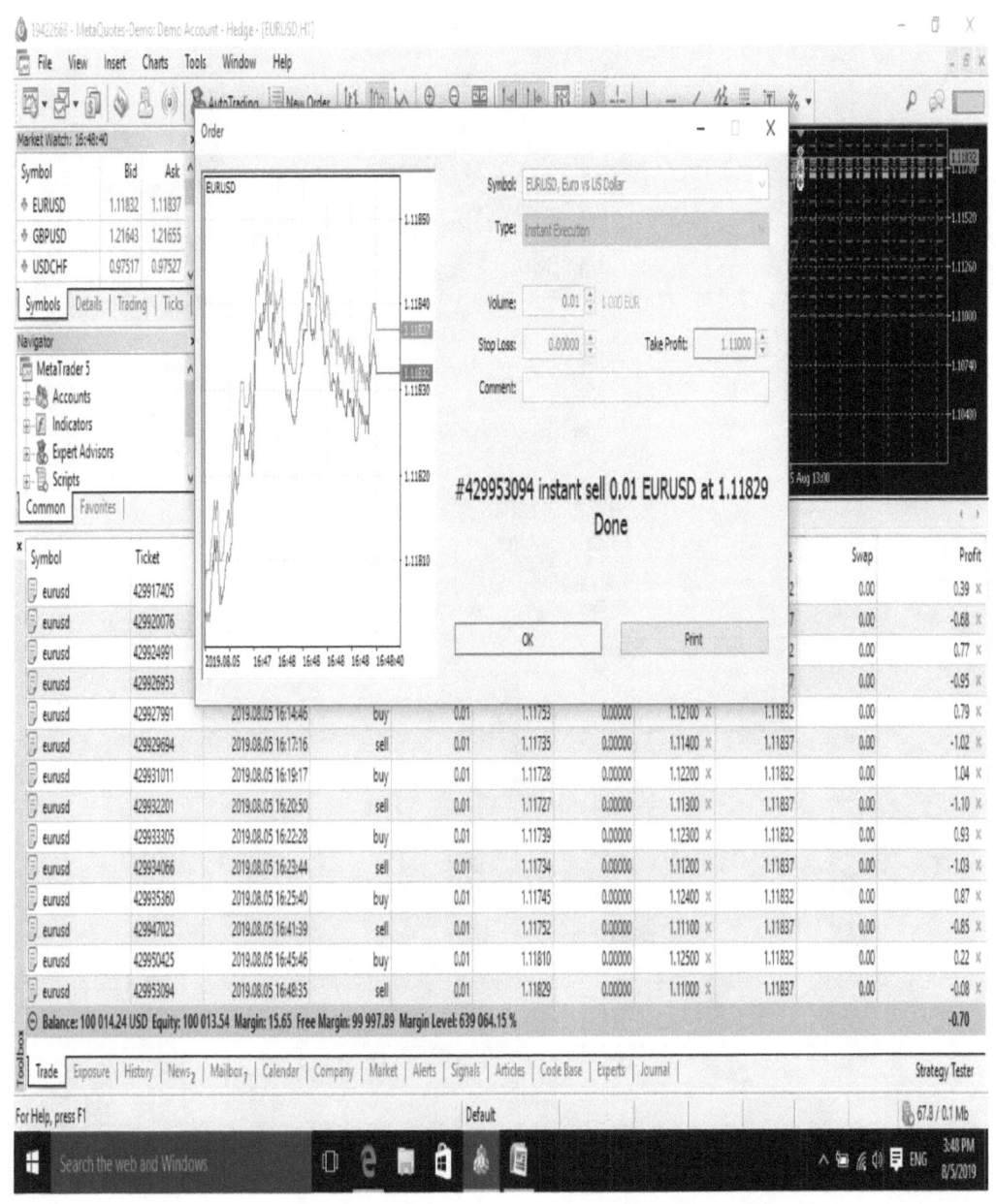

The 15th order is a buy order placed at the current price of 1.1182 and a take profit limit of approximately 80 pips at 1.1260.

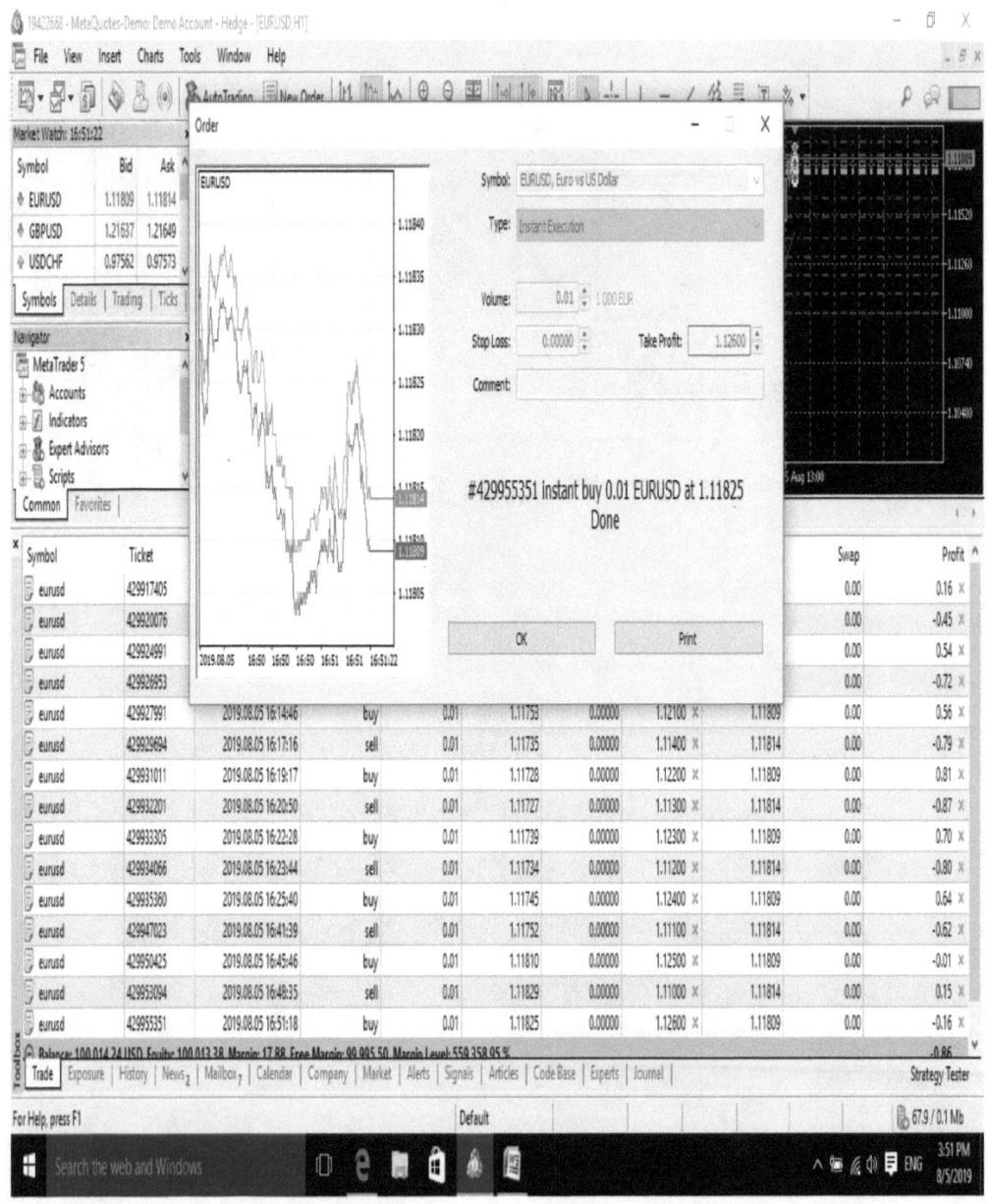

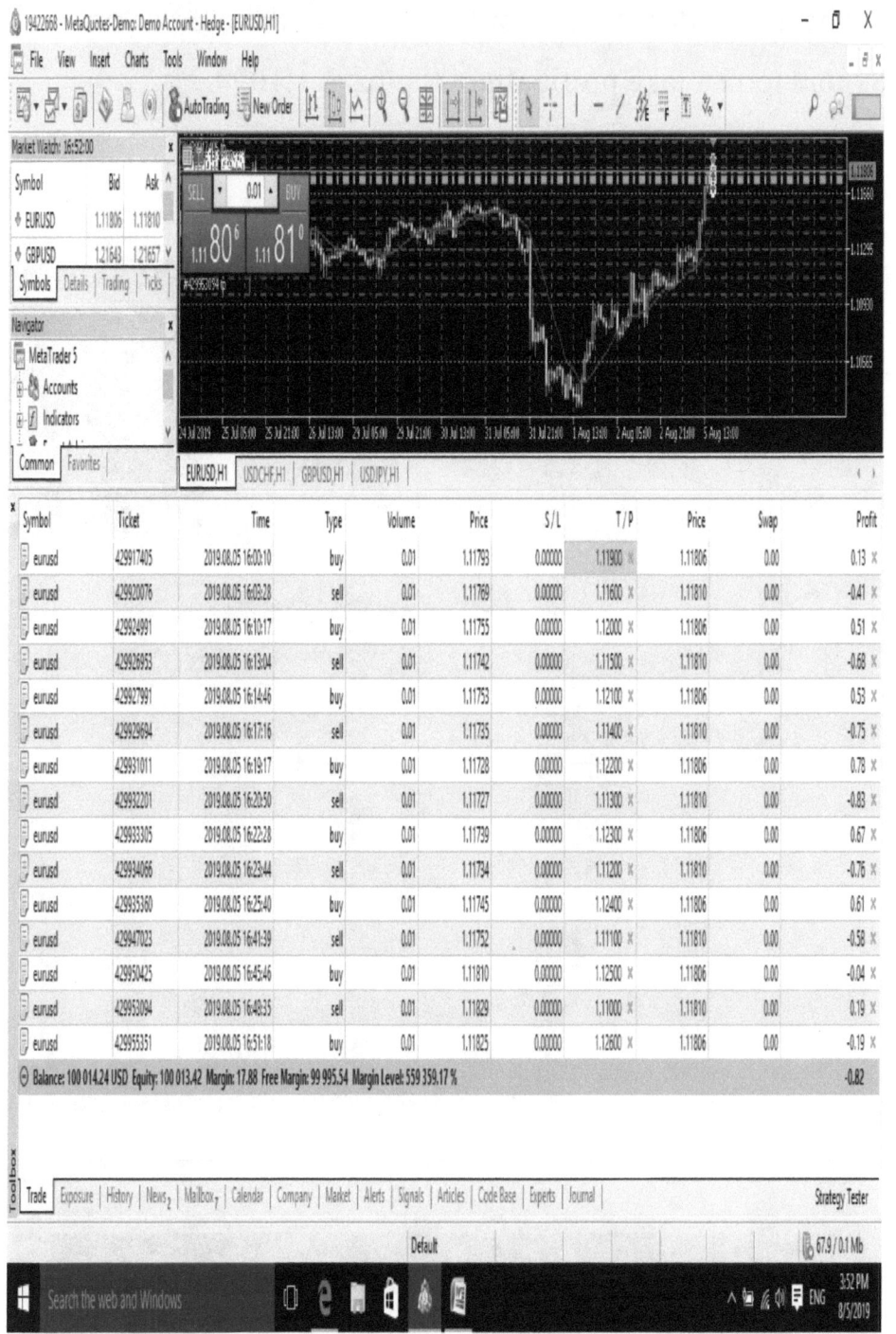

Now we have fifteen orders, eight to buy and seven to sell.

The 16th order is a sell order placed at the current price of 1.1181 and took a take profit after 90 pips at 1.1090.

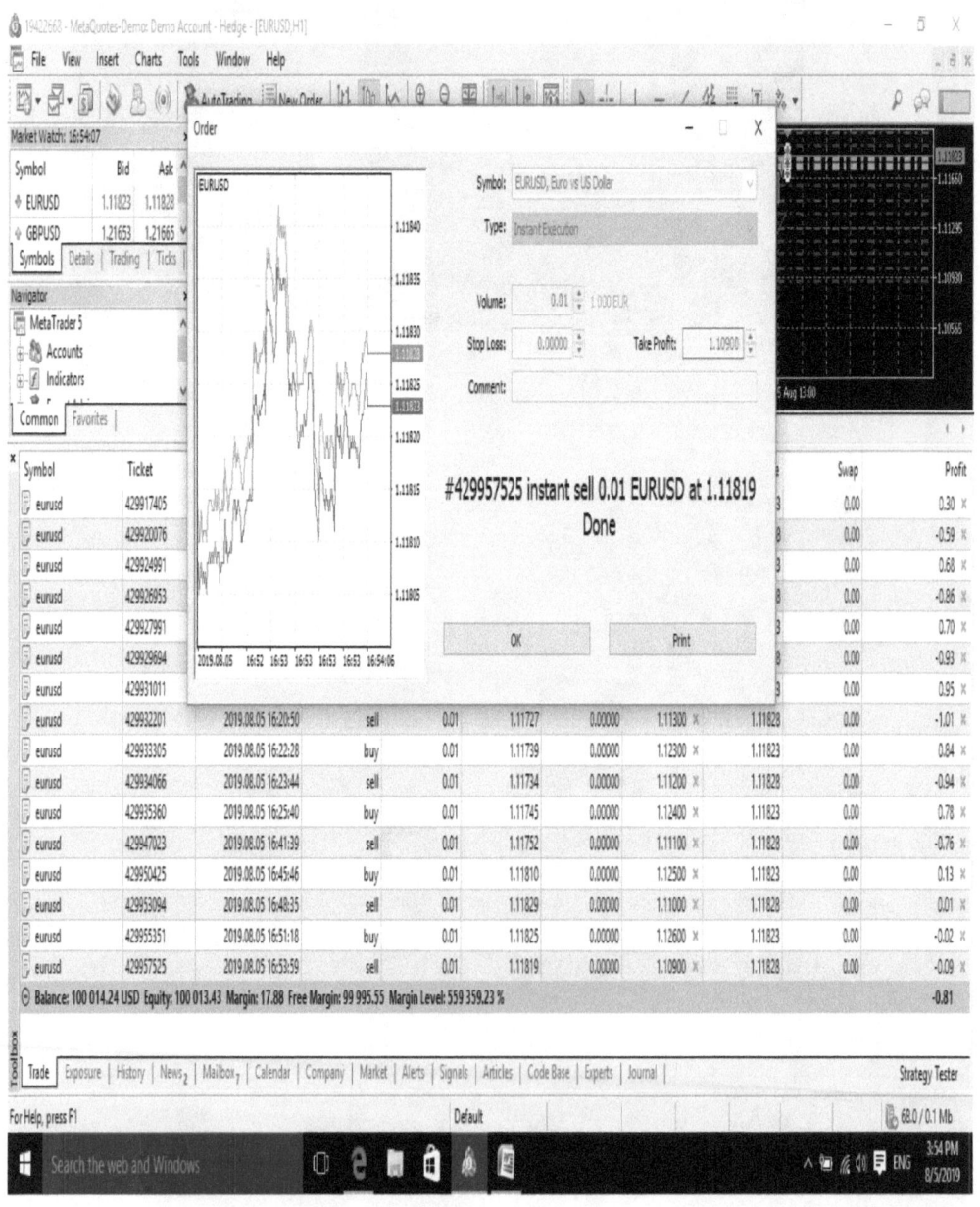

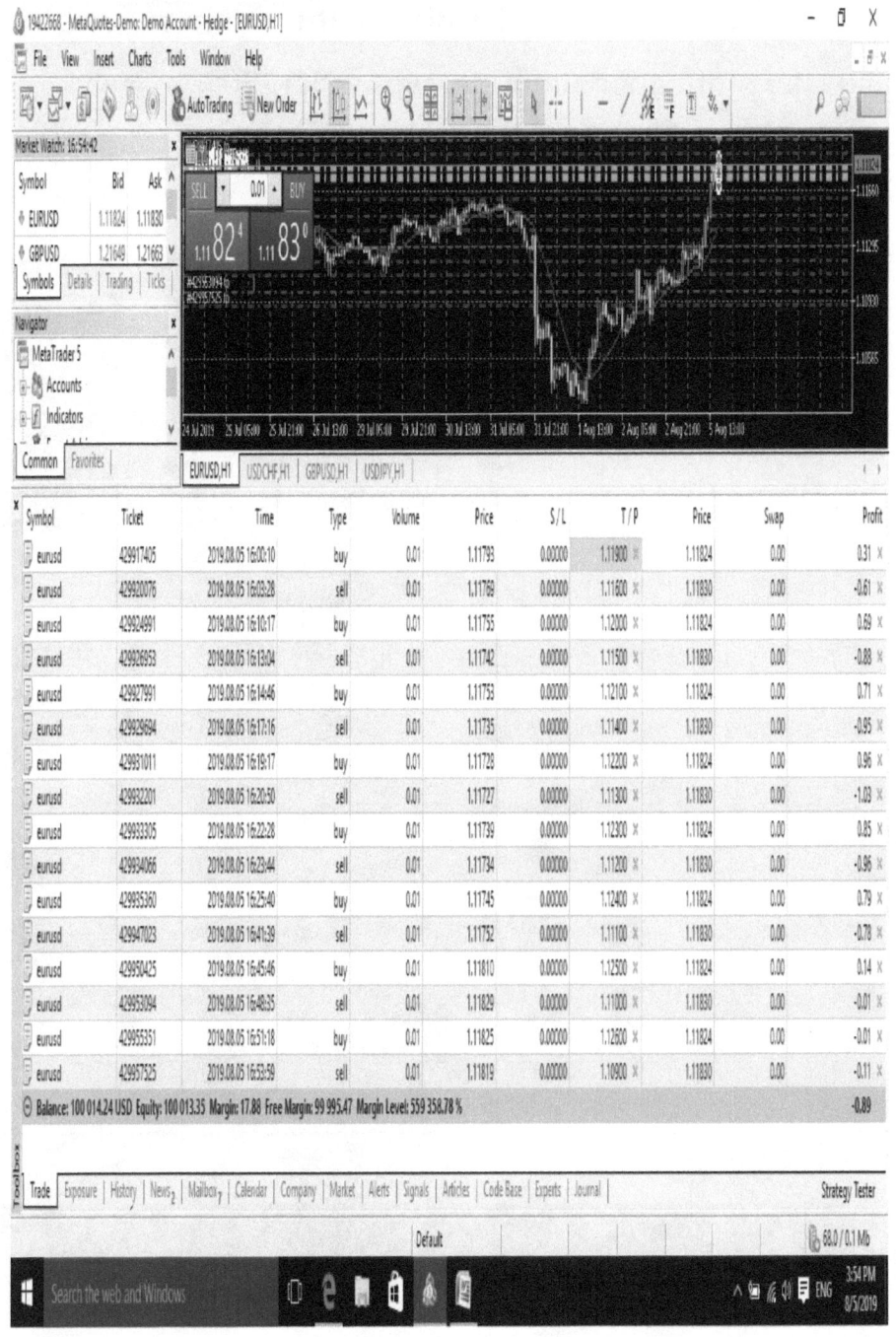

Now we have sixteen orders, eight to buy and eight to sell.

The 17th order is a buy order placed at the current price of 1.1183 and take profit after almost 90 pips at 1.1270.

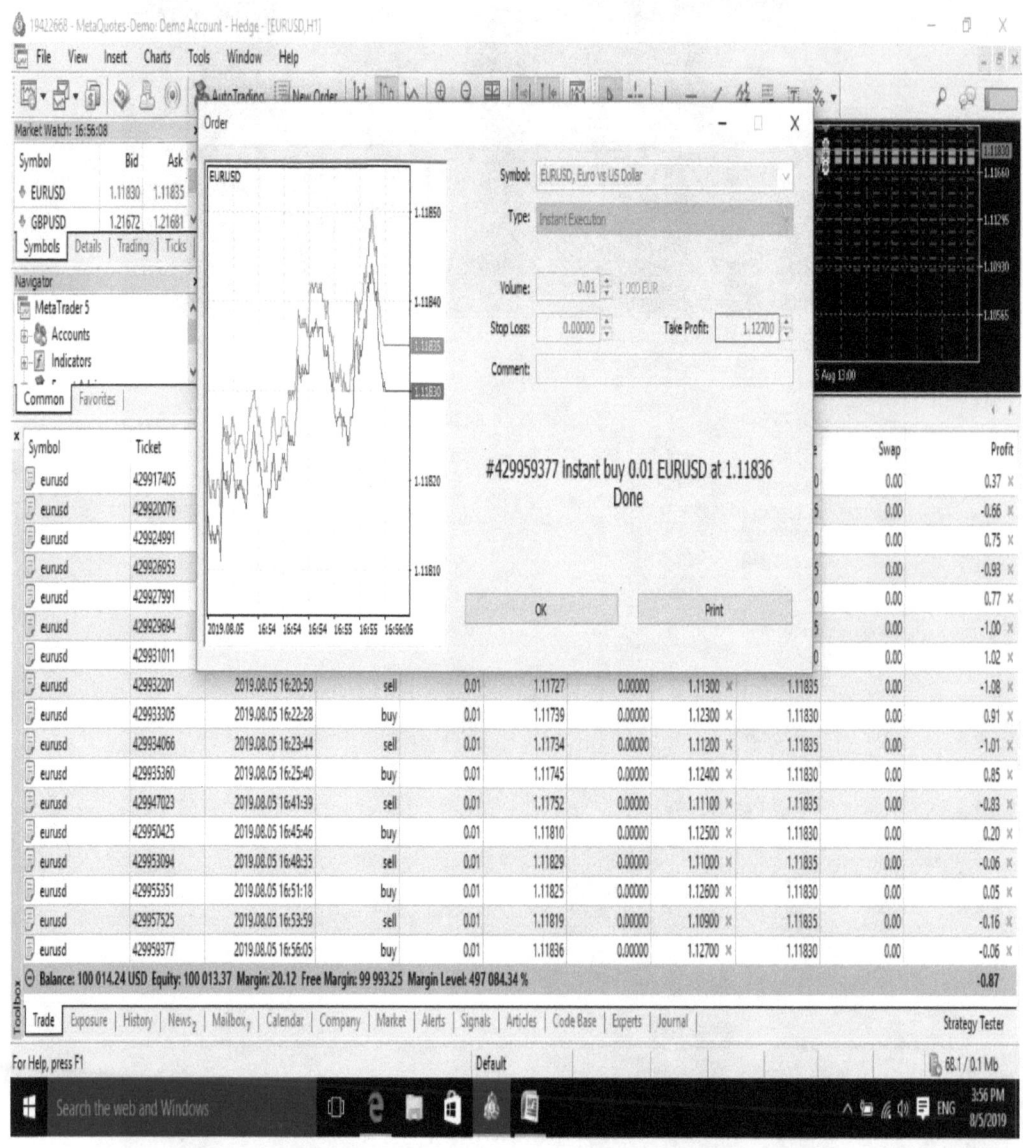

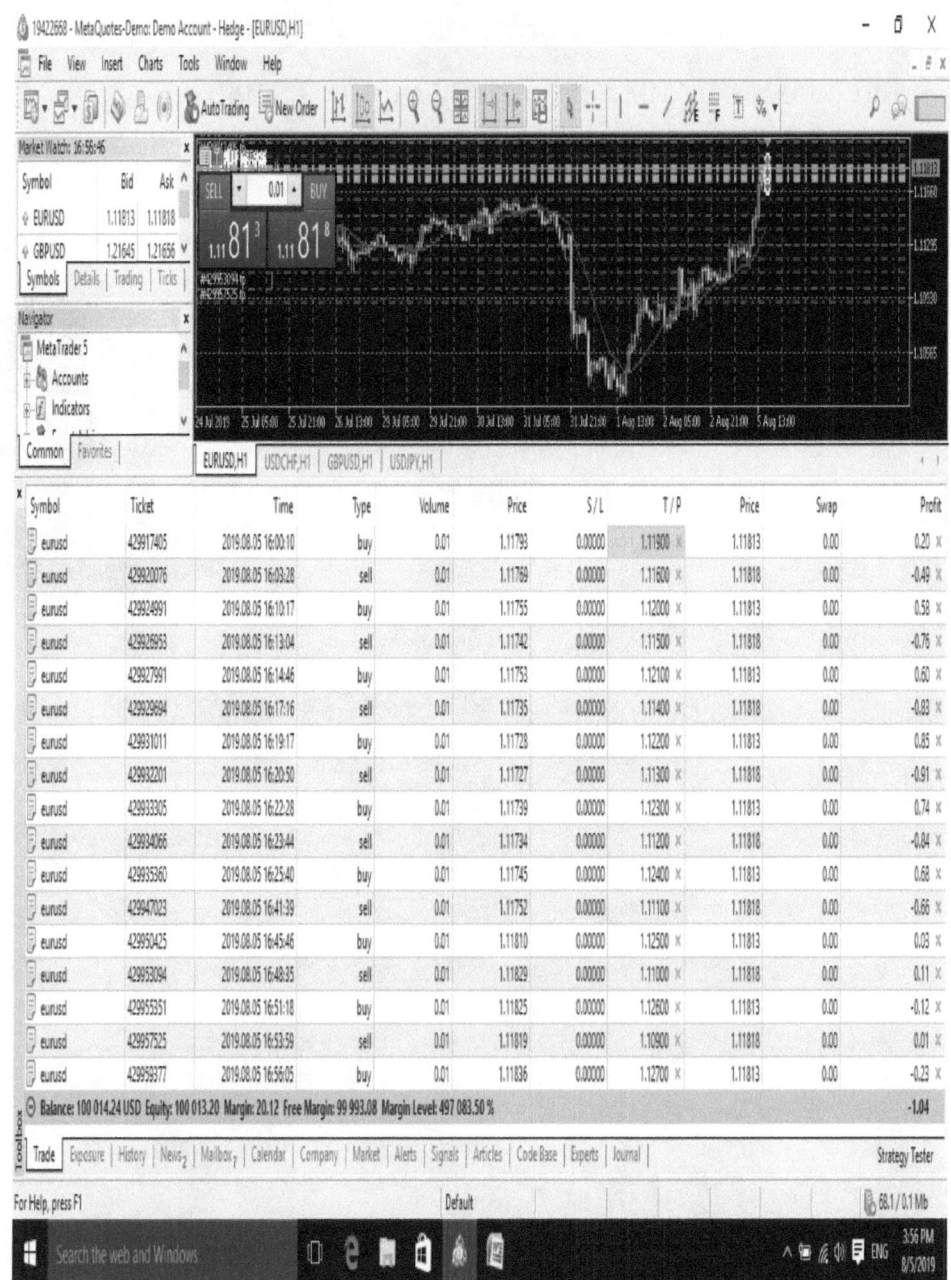

Now we have seventeen orders, nine buy orders and eight sell orders.

The 18th order is a sell order placed at the current price of 1.1179 and take profit after almost 100 pips at 1.1080.

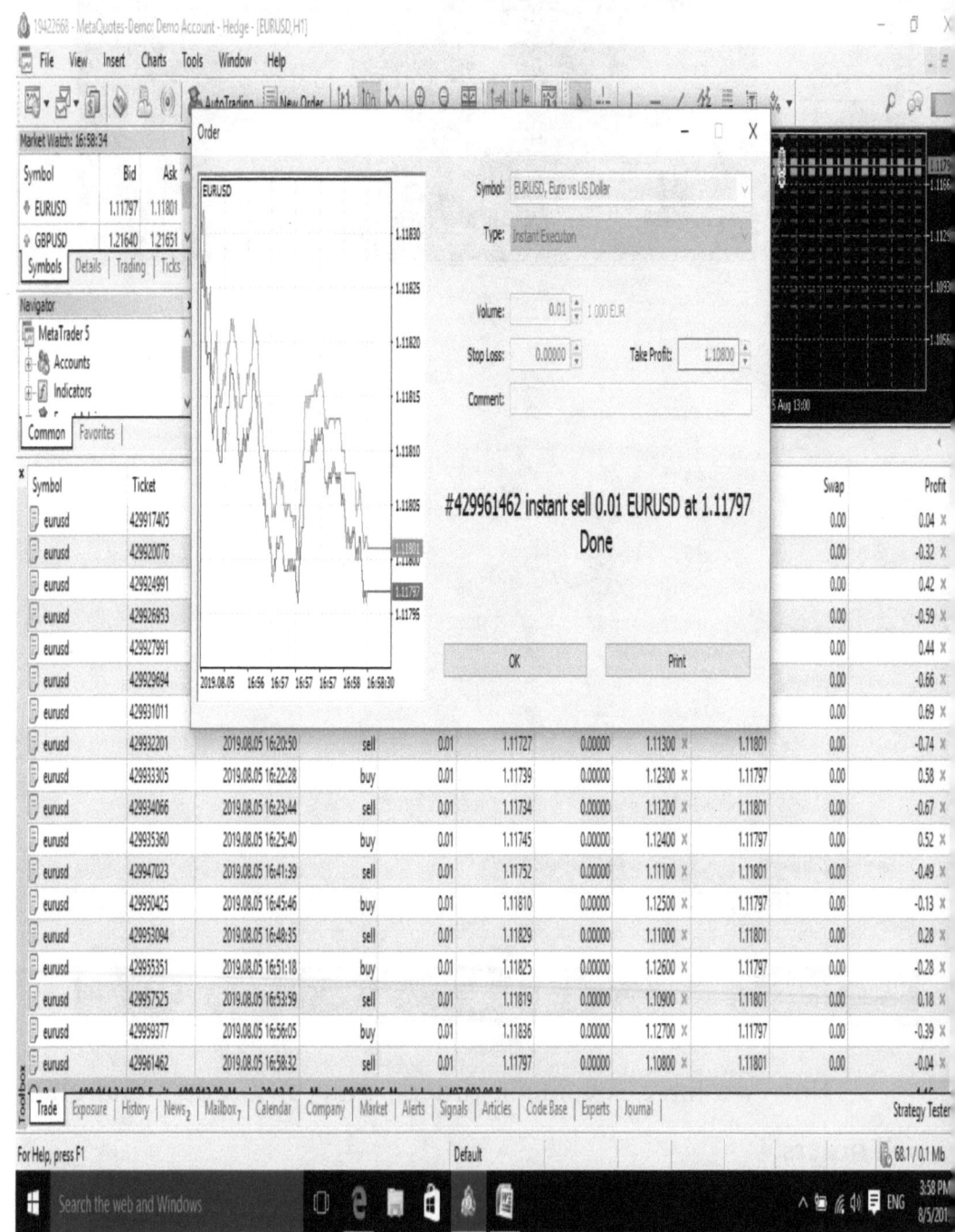

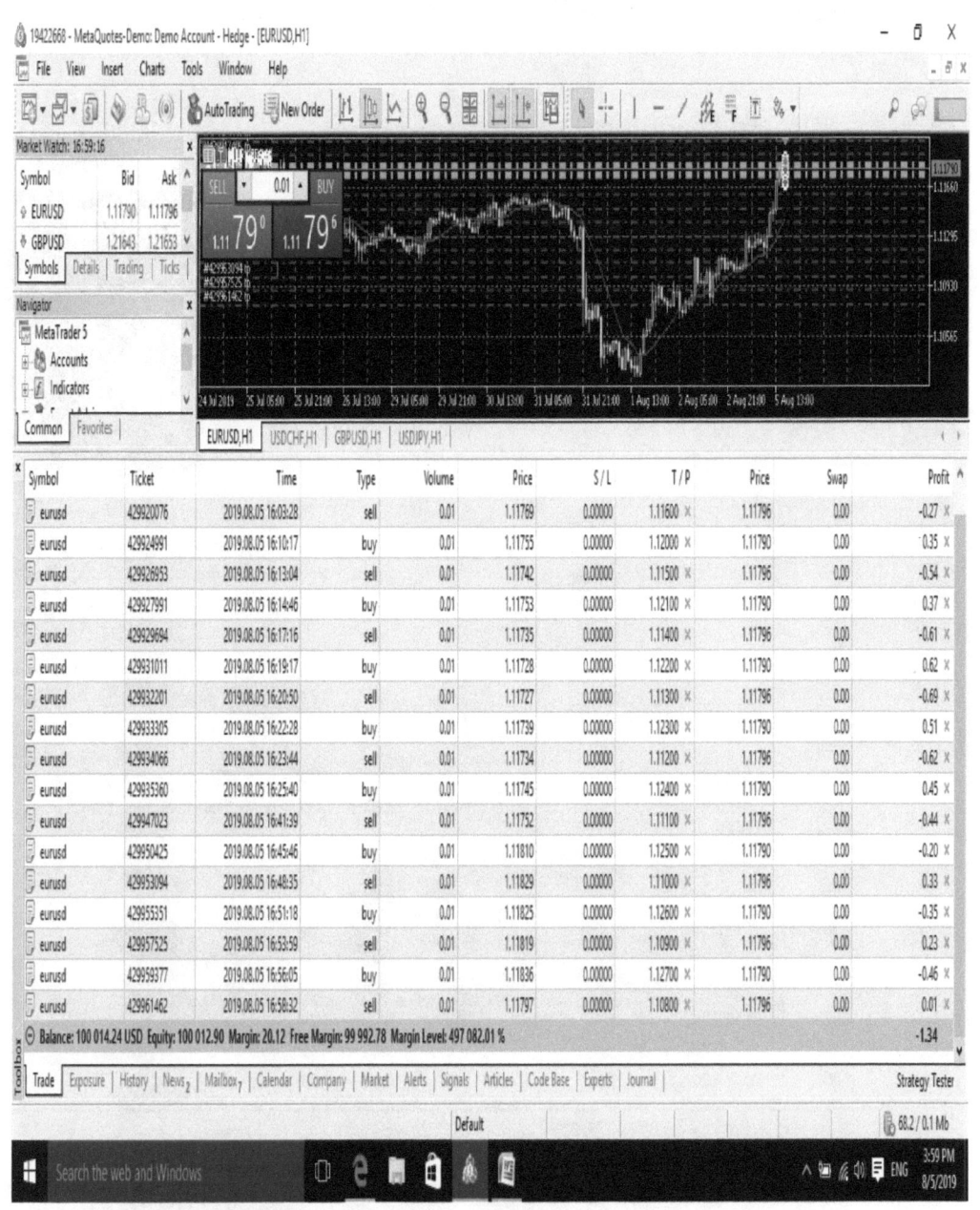

Now we have eighteen orders, nine to buy and nine to sell.

The 19th order is a buy order placed at the current price of 1.1184 and take profit after 95 pips around 1.1280.

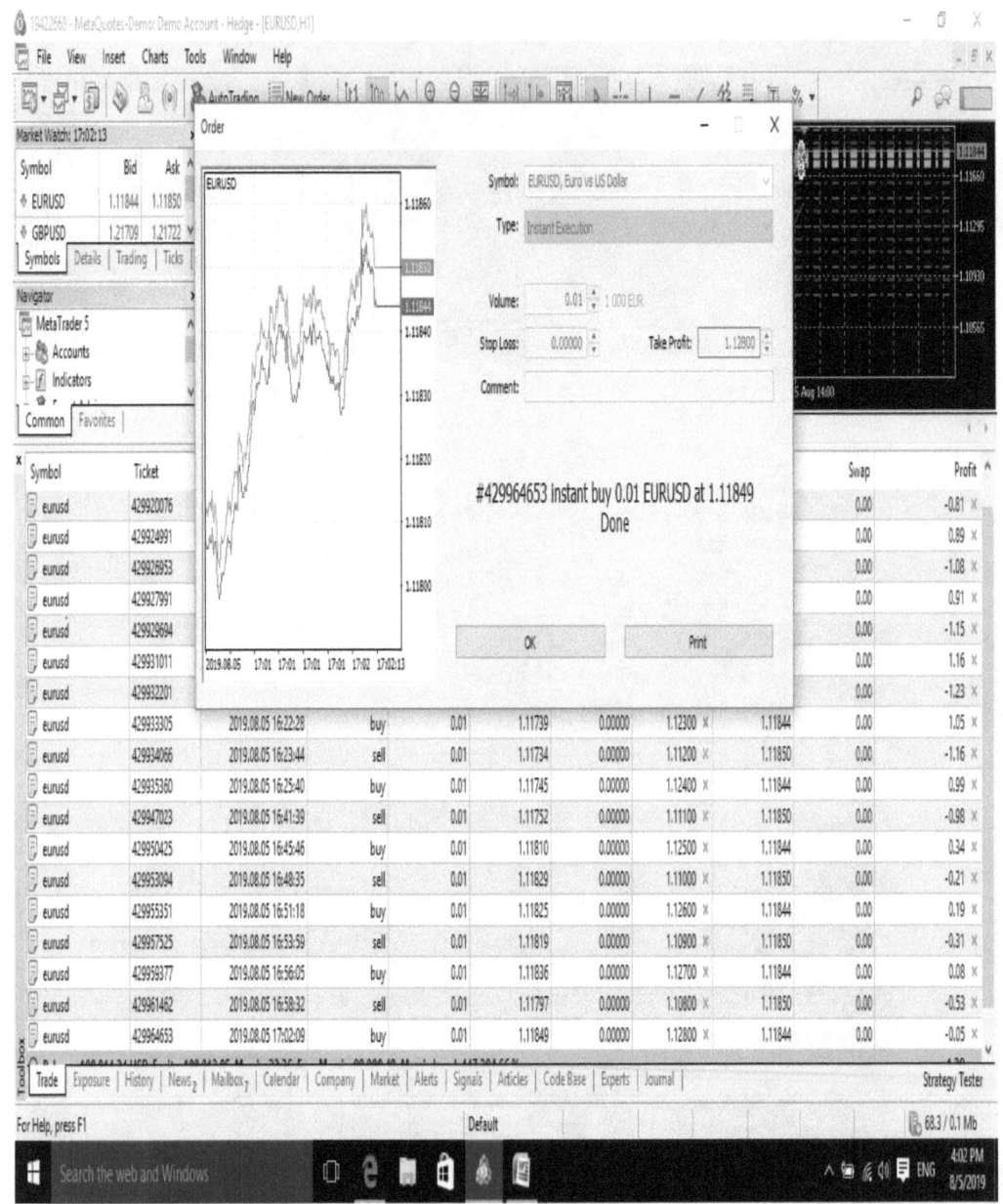

The 20th order is a sell order placed at the current price of 1.1183 and take profit after almost 110 pips at 1.1070.

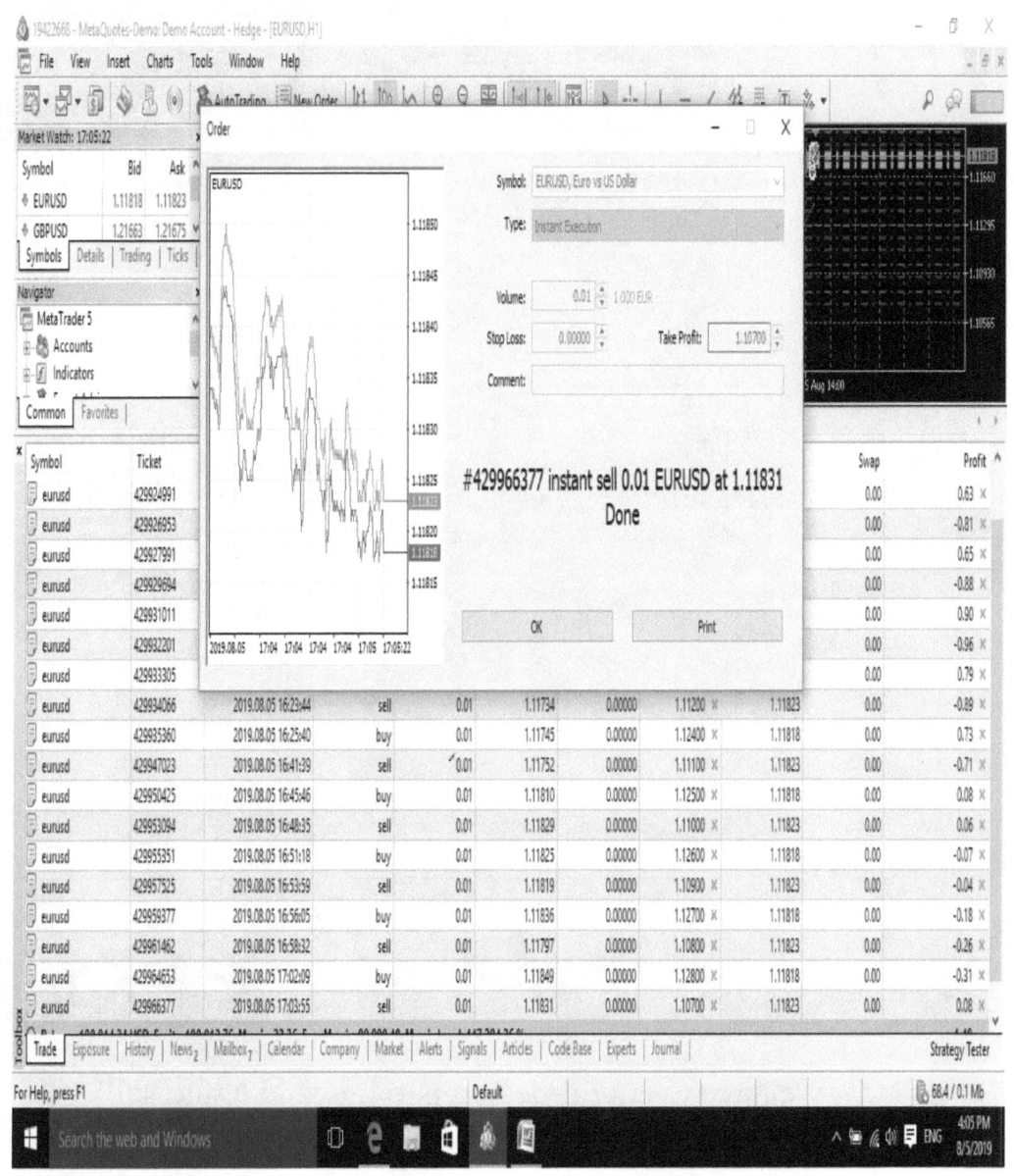

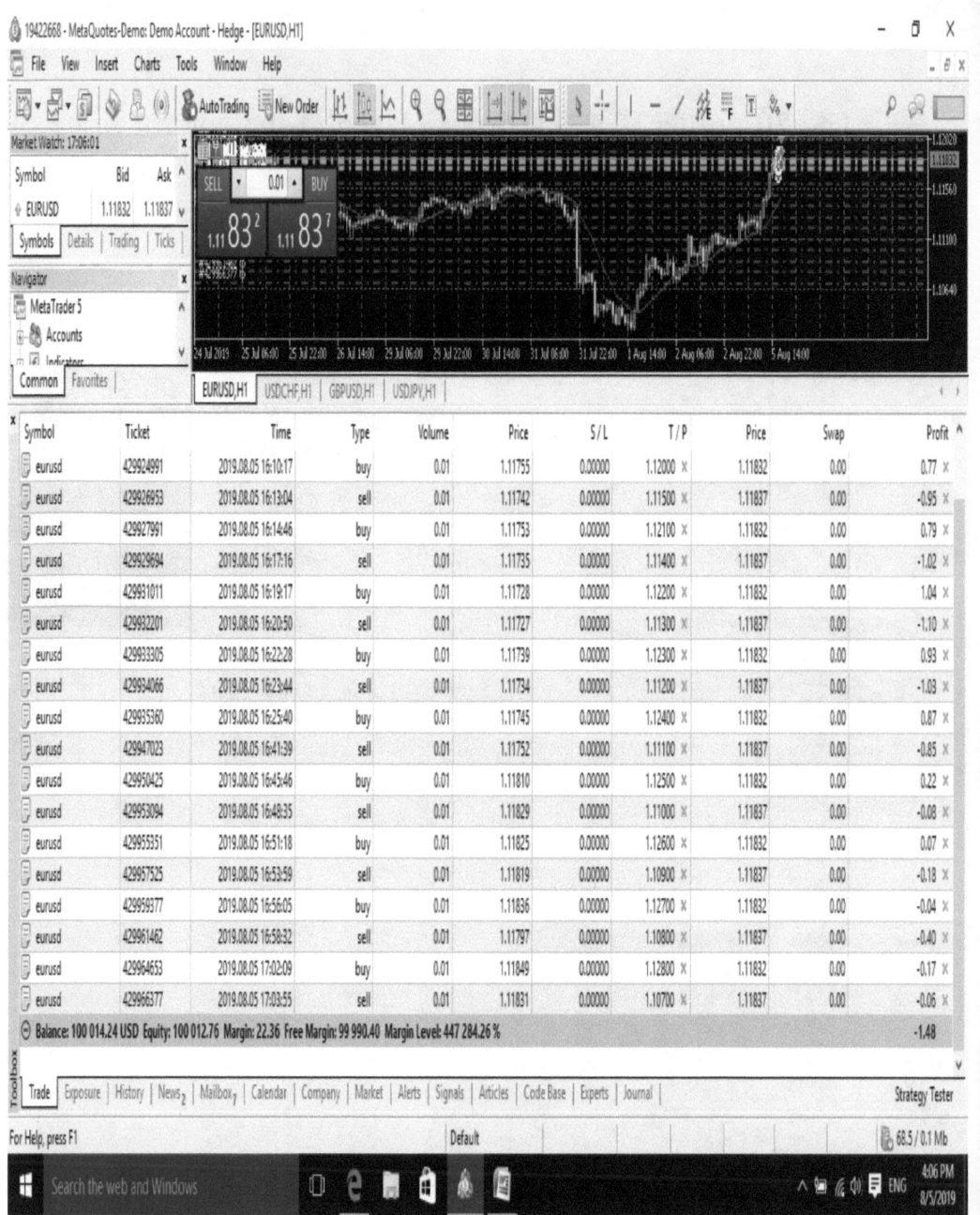

Now we have twenty orders, ten to buy and ten to sell.

Making Profits

By reviewing the situation now we find that there are buy orders that started to make profits. The first strategy also made profits on three buy orders.

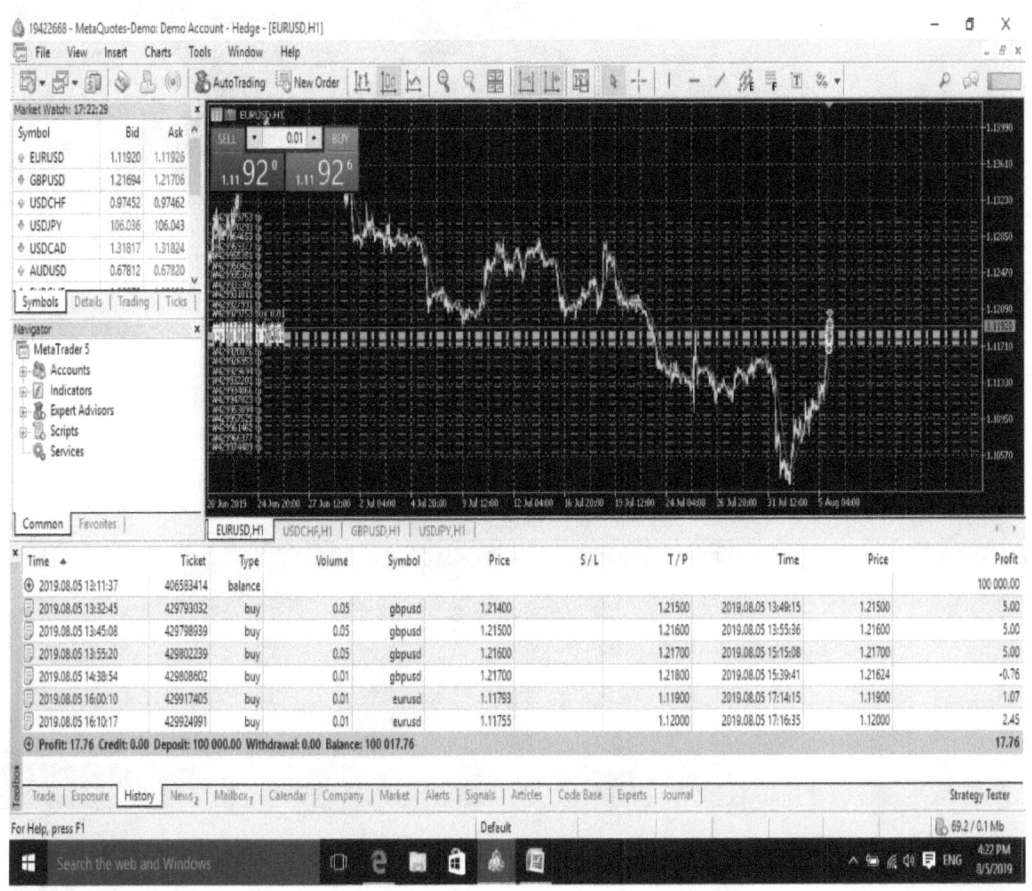

In the following figure, we found that more profits have been made.

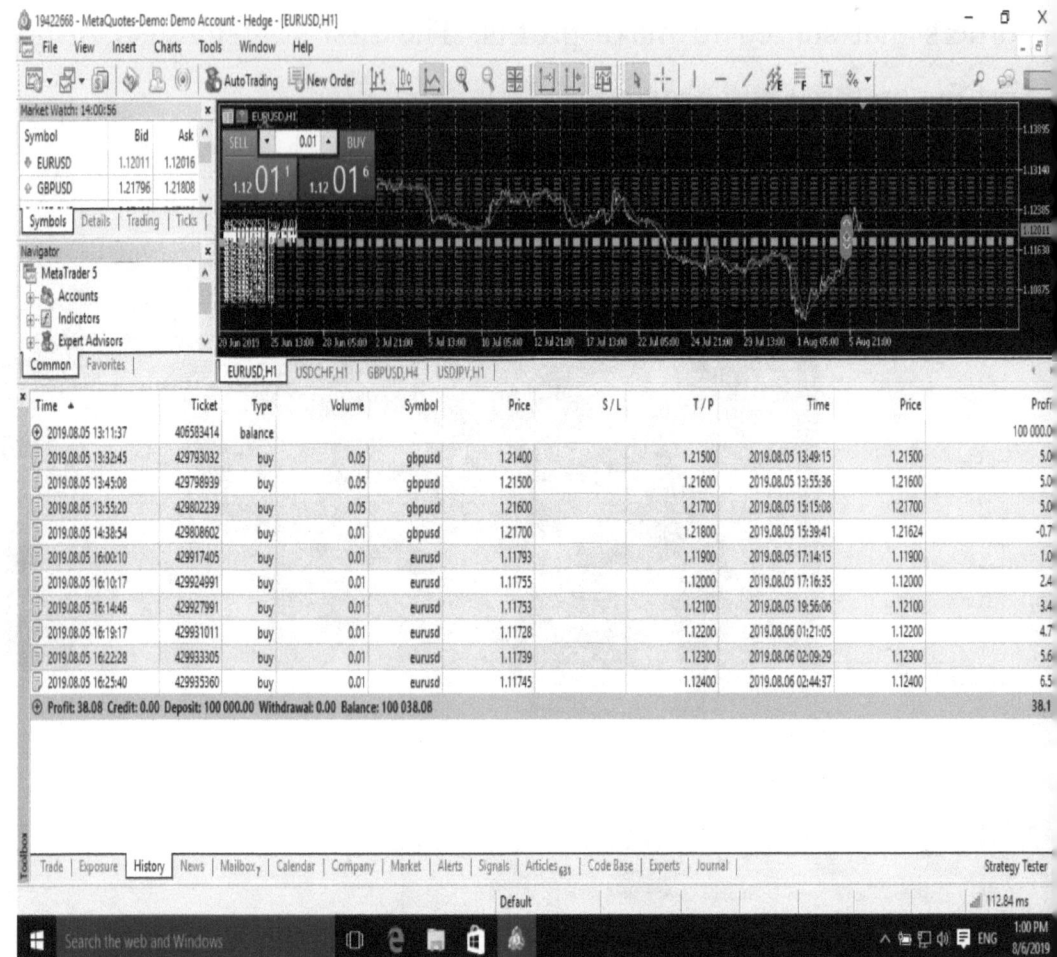

Probabilities of profit and loss

After placing a set of buy and sell orders and take profit limits, a range of probabilities can occur:

1. If the price tends to go up, buy orders will begin to make profit.

2. If the price tends to go down, the sell orders will start to make profit.

3 - If the price tends to rise and then return to go down, profit will be achieved from both buy and sell orders.

4. If the indicator moves up and closed all buy orders and then turns down and closed all sell orders, profits from all of them are achieved and this is considered the best position that can be achieved from this strategy.

5. All orders can be closed at any time if a profitable situation is achieved.

6. The only problem in this strategy is the continuation of the price to move in one direction, either up or down.

Conclusion

Now that the details of both strategies have been explained in terms of how they are implemented, how we are dealing with and how to maximize profits, I would like to make a few comments.

First, this strategy aims to making profit during both the rise and fall of the price with no need to predict whether the price will rise or fall. This may be right or wrong, despite the long years that I have spent in research and experimentation, and although all positive results that have been achieved most often. Second, although this strategy does not rely on predicting the rise or fall of the price, it may be useful during the use of this strategy to rely on technical and fundamental analysis to obtain results that can enhance the use of this strategy. Although this strategy, in my view, leads to an unprecedented increase in profitability, it must be handled with caution and tried again and again through demo accounts.

Third, if we make a quick comparison between the two strategies, we may find that the first strategy has more advantages due to many reasons. The pending orders leads to saving money which can be exhausted in instant execution orders; they can be closed at any time without incurring charges of spread, as well as avoiding the risk of moving in one direction.

However, further research, study and experimentation are required in order to avoid the negative aspects of this strategy in order to maximize profits and achieving more perfect results.

Good Luck

The Author

nasser4@hotmail.com

Disclaimer

No responsibility for loss occasioned to any person or corporate body acting or refraining to act as a result of reading material in this book can be accepted by the Publisher or by the Author.

www.ingramcontent.com/pod-product-compliance
Lightning Source LLC
Chambersburg PA
CBHW030726180526
45157CB00008BA/3061